ENGLISH
18TH
CENTURY
COOKERY

THE LIVING PAST

0 – 905694 – 41 – 4

PRINTED IN ROMANIA

ENGLISH 18TH CENTURY COOKERY

Illustrated by Cecilia Ware

 Contents

Foreword

During the eighteenth century, English cookery was deeply influenced by the development of foreign trade, and many of the recipes and notes in this book illustrate the lasting quality of that influence. Many are still favourites today, yet others have somehow been forgotten. Certainly the quantities are often overwhelming, the directions not always precise and indeed sometimes the ingredients are not suitable for present-day use. Nonetheless the able cook need not be disheartened – commonsense and a little imagination are all that is required to adapt some of these ideas into delicious realities.

The present collection of recipes is culled from an old household library, and much of their charm lies in the way they were originally presented. In view of this, spelling and punctuation have been changed only where the meaning of the original was somewhat obscure, and a glossary has been provided to explain the less familiar terms which are indicated in the text by a number.

Nowadays an increasing interest, both practical and historical is being shown in genuine old recipes and, although immediate success cannot in every case be guaranteed, whatever the reader's approach there is much in these pages to delight and stimulate the senses.

Note: At the time of the original publication of these recipes standards of hygiene and ingredients in common use were often of a rather dubious nature, and some of the recipes in this book fall far short of modern-day standards. The Publishers can take responsibility only for the authenticity of these recipes; wherever there is any possibility that the methods and ingredients involved might be harmful to health, please seek the advice of an expert.

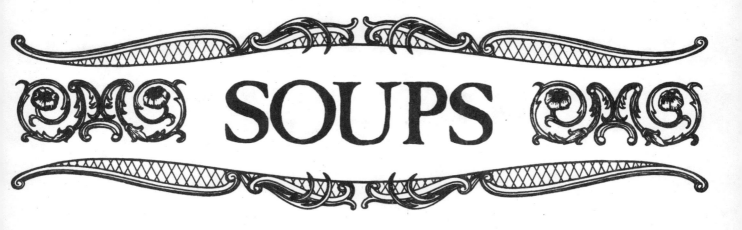

SOUPS

TO MAKE A TUREEN OF SOUP FLEMISH FASHION

Scald[1] half a dozen of turkey pinions[2], four sheep's rumps, and ½ a pound or more of pickled pork; then tie up each sort together, scald also a good savoy[3] cut into quarters and tied; put them altogether into a pan with good broth, a faggot of sweet herbs, parsley, green shalots, 3 cloves, pepper and salt; boil slowly; when done, drain the meat; put it into the tureen, and serve a good gravy sauce with it.

TO MAKE CURRY

Take the skin off two chickens; carve, wash and dry them; put them in a stew-pan with a tea-cupful of water, salt, and a few onions, and stew them with a few green peas, or the egg plant, till tender; then take a lump of butter, the size of a pigeon's egg, a little mace, Cayenne pepper to taste, a tea-spoonful each of fresh turmeric and cardamoms, pounded with a shalot in a marble mortar; roll these ingredients with a little flour in the butter, and dissolve them in the stew. If the curry is to be brown, it must be fried a little before the curry-ball is added to the gravy.

TO MAKE SOUP MAIGRE[4]

Take of veal, beef cut into small pieces, and scrag of mutton, 1 pound each; put them into a saucepan with 2 quarts of water; put into a clean cloth, 1 ounce of barley, an onion, a small bundle of sweet herbs, 3 or 4 heads of celery cut small, a little mace, 2 or 3 cloves, 3 turnips pared and cut in two, a large carrot cut into small pieces, and a young lettuce. Cover the pot close, and let it stew very gently for six hours. Then take out the spice, sweet herbs, and onion, and pour all into a soup dish, seasoned with salt.

TO MAKE PORTABLE SOUP

Cut into small pieces 3 large legs of veal, 1 of beef, and the lean part of a ham: lay the meat in a large cauldron, with a quarter of a pound of butter at the bottom, 4 ounces of anchovies, and 2 ounces of mace. Cut small 6 heads of clean washed celery, freed from green leaves, and put them into the cauldron, with 3 large carrots cut thin. Cover all close, and set it on a moderate fire. When the gravy begins to draw, keep taking it off till it is all extracted. Then cover the meat with water, let it boil gently for four hours, then strain it through a hair sieve into a clean pan till it is reduced to one third. Strain the gravy drawn from the meat into a pan, and let it boil gently, until it be of a glutinous consistence. Take care and skim off all the fat as it rises. Watch it when it is nearly done, that it does not burn; next season it with Cayenne pepper, and pour it on flat earthen dishes, a quarter of an inch thick. Let it stand till the next day, and then cut it out by round tins larger than a crown piece. Set the cakes in dishes in the sun to dry, and turn them often. When fully dried, put them into a tin box with a piece of clean white paper between each, and keep them in a dry place. If made in frosty weather it will soon become solid. This kind of soup is exceedingly convenient for private families, for by putting one of the cakes in a saucepan with about a pint of water, and a little salt, a basin of good broth may be made in a few minutes. It will likewise make an excellent gravy for roast turkeys, fowls, and game.

TO MAKE MOCK TURTLE SOUP

Scald[1] a calf's head with the skin on, and take off the horny part, which cut into two-inch square pieces; clean and dry them well in a cloth, and put them into a stew-pan, with 4 quarts of water made as follows: take 6 or 7 pounds of beef, a calf's foot, a shank of ham, an onion, 2 carrots, a turnip, a head of celery, some cloves, and whole pepper, a bunch of sweet herbs, a little lemon peel, and a few truffles. Put these into 8 quarts of water, and stew them gently till the liquid is reduced one half; then strain it off and put it into the stew-pan, with the horny parts of the calf's head. Add some knotted marjoram, savoury, thyme, parsley chopped small, with some cloves and mace pounded, a little Cayenne pepper, some green onions, a shalot cut fine, a few chopped mushrooms, and half a pint of Madeira wine. Stew these gently till the soup is reduced to two quarts, then heat a little broth; mix some flour, smoothing it with the yolks of two eggs, and stir it over a gentle fire till it is near boiling. Add this to the soup; keep stirring as you pour it in, and continue stewing for another hour. When done, squeeze in the juice of half a lemon, half an orange, and throw in some boiled force-meat balls. Serve it up in a tureen hot. This soup is deliciously gratifying and nutritive.

TO MAKE ASPARAGUS SOUP

Put a small broiled bone to a pint and a half of peas, and water in proportion, a root of celery, a small bunch of sweet herbs, a large onion, Cayenne pepper and salt to taste; boil it briskly for five hours, strain and pulp it; then add a little spinach juice and asparagus boiled and cut into small pieces. A tea-spoonful of walnut soy, and a tea-spoonful of mushroom catsup, answers as well as the bone.

WHITE SOUP

Stew a knuckle of veal and a scrag of mutton three or four hours, with spice; strain it; blanch ½ a pound of sweet almonds, beat them with a spoonful or two of cream to prevent their oiling; put them with a pint of cream into the soup, stir it, and give it a boil;

strain it through a cloth, squeeze the almonds as dry as possible, heat it again, and thicken it as a custard with eggs; put a toasted roll in the tureen, and pour the soup over it. If there is a breast of cold fowl or veal, less almonds will do; if the meat be stewed and strained the day before, it does much better.

CHARITABLE SOUP

Take the liquor of meat boiled the day before, with the bones of leg and shin of beef; add to the liquor as much as will make 130 quarts, also the meat of 10 stones of leg and shin of beef, and 2 ox heads, all cut in pieces; add 2 bunches of carrots, 4 bunches of turnips, 2 bunches of leeks, ½ a peck[5] of onions, 1 bunch of celery, ¼ a pound of pepper, and some salt. Boil it for six hours. Either oatmeal or barley may be put in to thicken it, if thought necessary. This soup may be used at any gentleman's table.

TO MAKE VEAL GRAVY SOUP

Garnish the bottom of the stew-pan with thin pieces of lard, then a few slices of ham, slices of veal cutlet, sliced onions, carrots, parsnips, celery, a few cloves upon the meat, and a spoonful of broth; soak it on the fire in this manner till the veal throws out its juice; then put it on a stronger fire, till the meat catches to the bottom of the pan, and is brought to a proper colour: then add a sufficient quantity of light broth, and simmer it on a slow fire till the meat is thoroughly done; add a little thyme and mushrooms. Skim and sift it clear for use.

TO MAKE A TUREEN OF HODGE-PODGE OF DIFFERENT SORTS

Take either a brisket of beef, mutton, steaks, whole pigeons, rabbits cut in quarters, veal, or poultry; boil a long time over a slow fire in a short liquid, with some onions, carrots, parsnips, tulips[6], celery, a faggot of parsley, green shalots, 1 clove of garlick, 3 of spices, a laurel leaf[7], thyme, a little basil, large thick sausages, and thin broth or water; when done, drain the meat, and place it upon a dish intermixed

with roots, sift and skim the sauce, reduce some of it to a glaze, if desired; glaze the meat with it, then add some gravy on the same stew-pan, and broth sufficient to make sauce enough with pepper and salt: sift it in a sieve, and serve upon the meat. If brisket of beef is used, let it be half done before putting in the roots, which should be scalded[1] first as this makes the broth more palatable.

BEEF GRAVY SOUP

Cut slices of lean beef, according to the quantity wanted, which place in a stew-pan, upon sliced onions and roots, adding two spoonsful of fat broth; soak this on a slow fire for half an hour, stirring it well; when it catches a proper colour, add thin broth made of suitable herbs, with a little salt over it.

A POOR MAN'S SOUP

Pick a handful of parsley leaves, mince them fine, and strew over a little salt; shred six green onions, and put them with the parsley in a sauce-boat. Add three table-spoonsful of oil and vinegar with some pepper and salt.

A CHEAP RICE AND MEAT SOUP

Put a pound of rice and a little pepper and broth herbs, into two quarts of water; cover them close, and simmer very softly; put in a little cinnamon, two pounds of good ox cheek, and boil the whole till the goodness is incorporated by the liquor.

Another Cheap Soup

Take an ox cheek, two pecks[5] of potatoes, a quarter of a peck of onions, three-quarters of a pound of salt, and an ounce and a half of pepper – to be boiled in ninety pints of water, on a slow fire until reduced to sixty. A pint of this soup, with a small piece of meat, is a good meal for a hearty working man. Some of every vegetable, with a few herbs, may be added.

HERRING SOUP

Take eight gallons of water, and mix it with five pounds of barley-meal. Boil it to the consistence of a thick jelly. Season it with salt, pepper, vinegar, sweet herbs, and, to give it a gratifying flavour, add the meat of four red herrings pounded.

TO MAKE JELLY BROTH

Put into the stew-pan, slices of beef, veal fillet, a fowl, and one or two partridges, according to the quantity required. Put it on the fire without liquid, until it catches a little, and add the meat now and then. To give it a proper colour, add some good clear boiling broth and scalded[1] roots such as carrots, turnips, parsnips, parsley roots, celery, large onions, two or three cloves, a small bit of nutmeg and whole pepper; boil it on a slow fire about four or five hours with attention; and add a few cloves of garlic or shalots, and a small faggot, or bunch of parsley and thyme tied together. When it is of a good yellow colour, sift it; it serves for sauces, and adds strength to the soups.

TO PREPARE A NUTRITIOUS SOUP

A pound of Scotch barley, with sufficient time allowed in the cooking, will make a gallon of water into a tolerable pudding consistency. A pint basin filled with it will hold a spoon upright, when at its proper degree of warmth for eating. Thoroughly steeped, it will produce a rich pulp, the form of the grains being nearly lost. Five hours' exposure in a moderately heated oven, will be sufficient; and it may be improved by an hour or two more.

Amongst other means for such preparation, when a baker's oven has been emptied of its bread, a pan of one gallon size may be put in to steep its contents during the preceding night, and then renewing the usual baking in the morning. What has been lost by evaporation, may be renewed by the addition of warm water. All the seasoning requisite to make it as savory as plain family dishes generally are, will be about three large onions, one ounce of salt, and a quarter of an ounce of pepper. This seasoning should be put in before sending it to the oven.

TO MAKE COOLING BROTH

The herbs, fruits, seeds, flowers, or roots which are employed for cooling broth, are purslain[8], lettuces, chervil, leeks, borage, burnet[9], sorrel, garden and wild endive, bugloss[10], hop-tops, cos lettuces, young nettles, cucumbers, tops of elder, dandelion, liverwort[11], fumitory[12], beetroots, &c. Wash and chop a proper quantity, according to order, and boil a short time in thin veal or chicken broth; sift and keep it in a cool place. Warm it for use without boiling.

SAUCES

TO MAKE COMMON SAUCE

Soak slices of veal, ham, onions, parsnips, two cloves of garlic, two heads of cloves, then add broth, a glass of white wine, and two slices of lemon; simmer it over a slow fire, skim it well, and sift it; add three cloves of rocambole[13], bruised.

SWEET SAUCE

Mix two glasses of red wine, one of vinegar, three spoonsful of cullis[14], a bit of sugar, one sliced onion, a little cinnamon, and a laurel leaf[7]; boil them a quarter of an hour.

MISER'S SAUCE

Chop five or six large onions, mix a little verjuice[15] or vinegar, pepper, salt, and a little butter; serve it up either warm or cold.

PARSON'S SAUCE

Chop lemon peel very fine, with two or three pickled cucumbers, a bit of butter, salt, and coarse pepper, a little flour, with two spoonsful of catsup, and stew it on the fire without boiling.

NUN'S SAUCE

Put slices of veal and ham in a stew-pan with a spoonful of oil, two mushrooms, a faggot of parsley, a clove of garlic, two heads of cloves, half a leaf of laurel[7]; let it catch a little on the fire; then add some good broth, a little gravy, and some white wine; simmer it for some time, skim it well, and sift in a sieve. When ready, add two or three green shalots, and a dozen of pistachio nuts, whole.

PONTIFF'S SAUCE

Soak slices of veal, ham, sliced onions, carrots, parsnips, and a white head of celery: add a glass of white wine, as much good broth, a clove of garlic, four shalots, one clove, a little coriander, and two slices of peeled lemons. Boil on a slow fire till the meat is done; skim it and sift in a sieve; add a little catsup, and a small quantity of fine chopped parsley, just before it is used.

HOUSEWIFE'S SAUCE

Take some of the above sauce sifted without gravy, add a bit of butter rolled in flour, and chopped chervil: use it when warm.

TO MAKE SAUCE PIQUANTE

Put a bit of butter with two sliced onions into a stew-pan, with a carrot, a parsnip, a little thyme, laurel[7], basil, two cloves, two shalots, a clove of garlic, and some parsley; turn the whole over the fire until it be well coloured; then shake in some flour, and moisten it with some broth, and a spoonful of vinegar. Let it boil over a slow fire: skim and strain it through a sieve. Season it with salt and pepper, and serve it with any dish required to be heightened.

11

ADMIRAL'S SAUCE

Chop an anchovy, capers, and seven or eight green rocamboles[13]; simmer them on the fire with a little salt, pepper, grated nutmeg, and butter rolled in flour; when ready, add a lemon, squeezed.

NONPAREIL SAUCE

Take a slice of boiled ham, as much breast of roasted fowl, a pickled cucumber, a hard yolk of an egg, one anchovy, a little parsley, and a head of shalot, chopped very fine; boil it a moment in good catsup, and use it for meat or fish.

TO MAKE GRAVY CAKES

Chop two legs of beef in pieces, put them into a pot of water, stew it over a slow fire a day and a night; then add onions, herbs, and spices as for gravy; continue stewing it till the meat is off the bones, and the gravy quite out; then strain the liquor into a milk-pan, to which quantity it should be reduced; when cold, take off the fat, put it into a saucepan, and add whatever is required to flavour it; simmer it on a slow fire till reduced to about twelve saucers two-thirds full; put them in an airy place till as dry as leather, put them in paper bags, and keep them always in a dry place.

SAILOR'S SAUCE

Chop a fowl's liver with two or three shalots, and a couple of truffles or mushrooms; simmer these in a spoonful of oil, two or three spoonsful of gravy, a glass of white wine, a little salt and coarse pepper; simmer it about half an hour, and skim it very well before using.

QUEEN'S SAUCE

Simmer crumbs of bread in good gravy, until it is quite thick; take it off the fire, and add a few sweet almonds pounded, two hard yolks of eggs, and a breast of fowl roasted, all pounded very fine, boil a sufficien quantity of cream to your sauce, and sift it all togethe then add pepper and salt; and warm it without boiling

TO MAKE GENERAL'S SAUCE

To make this sauce properly, infuse all the followin ingredients for twenty-four hours, on ashes in a earthen pot, if possible, which must be very we stopped; viz., split six shalots, a clove of garlic, tw laurel leaves[7], thyme and basil in proportion, truffle tarragon leaves, half an ounce of mustard seed bruised six small pieces of Seville orange peel, a quarter of a ounce of cloves, as much mace, half an ounce of lon pepper[16], two ounces of salt; squeeze in a whole lemo and add half a glass of verjuice[15], five spoonsful o vinegar, and a pint of white wine; let it settle, and sif it very clear. This may be kept, bottled, a long time and it will serve for all sorts of meat and fish – bu it must be used in moderation.

CARACH SAUCE

Take three cloves of garlic, each cut in half, half a ounce of Cayenne pepper, and a spoonful or two eac of Indian soy and walnut pickle; mix it in a pint o vinegar, with as much cochineal as will colour it.

TO MAKE TOMATA CATSUP

Boil tomatas, full ripe, in their juice, to nearly th consistence of a pulp, pass them through a hair sieve and add salt to the taste. Aromatize it sufficiently wit clove, pepper, and nutmeg.

CATSUP FOR SEA STORE

Take a gallon of strong stale beer, a pound of anchovie washed from the pickle, the same of shalots peeled half an ounce of mace, half an ounce of cloves, a quarter of an ounce of whole pepper, three or fou large races[17] of ginger, and two quarts of large mush-room flaps, rubbed to pieces. Cover these close, and let it simmer till half wasted. Then strain it through a

flannel bag; let it stand till quite cold, and then bottle it. This may be carried to any part of the world; and a spoonful of it to a pound of fresh butter melted, will make a fine fish sauce, or will supply the place of gravy sauce. The stronger and staler the beer, the better will be the catsup.

Another

Chop twenty-four anchovies, having first boned them. Put to them ten shalots cut small, and a handful of scraped horse-radish, a quarter of an ounce of mace, a quart of white wine, a pint of water, and the same quantity of red wine; a lemon cut into slices, half a pint of anchovy liquor, twelve cloves, and the same number of peppercorns. Boil them together till it comes to a quart, then strain it off, cover it close and keep it in a cold dry place. Two spoonsful of it will be sufficient for a pound of butter. It is a good sauce for boiled fowls, or in the room of gravy, lowering it with hot water, and thickening it with a piece of butter rolled in flour.

TO MAKE CREAM SAUCE FOR A HARE

Run the cream over the hare or venison just before frothing it, and catch it in a dish; boil it up with the yolks of two eggs, some onion, and a piece of butter rolled in flour and salt. Half a pint of cream is the proportion for two eggs.

TO MAKE FISH SAUCE

Take walnuts at the season for pickling, slice them into an earthen pan, between every layer throw a small handful of salt, stir it with a wooden stirrer every day for a fortnight; strain the liquor through a coarse cloth, and let it stand to settle; pour off the clear, and boil it with a pound of anchovies to each pint; skim it, and let it stand to cool; give it another boil, add one pint of red port, and one of best white wine vinegar to each pint of liquor; also mace, cloves and nutmeg, of each half a quarter of an ounce, some flour of mustard, sliced horse-radish, and shalot or a clove of garlic in each bottle. Keep it well corked with a bladder tied over. The spice may be bruised or not, as desired, and a little whole black or Jamaica pepper may be added, as thought best.

Another

Take one pound of anchovies, a quart of claret, three-quarters of a pint of white wine vinegar, half an ounce of cloves and mace, two races[17] of ginger sliced, a little black pepper, the peel of a lemon, a piece of horse-radish, a large onion, a bunch of thyme and savory; set all these over a slow fire to simmer an hour, then strain it through a sieve; when cold, put it in a bottle with the spice, but not the herbs. To a large coffee-cupful cold, put a pound of butter; stir it over the fire till it is as thick as cream; shake the bottle when used, and put no water to the butter.

TO MAKE RAGOUT OF ASPARAGUS

Scrape one hundred of grass[18] clean; put them into cold water; cut them as far as is good and green, chop small two heads of endive, a young lettuce, and an onion. Put a quarter of a pound of butter into the stew-pan, and when it is melted, put in the grass with the other articles. Shake them well, and when they have stewed ten minutes, season them with a little pepper and salt; strew in a little flour, shake them about, and then pour in half a pint of gravy. Stew the whole till the sauce is very good and thick, and then pour all into the dish. Garnish with a few of the small tops of the grass.

The Same of Mushrooms

Broil on a gridiron[19] some large peeled mushrooms, and clean off the inside; when the outside is brown, put them into a stew-pan with a sufficient quantity of water to cover them; when they have stewed ten minutes, put to them a spoonful of white wine, the same of browning, and a little vinegar. Thicken it with butter and flour, give a gentle boil and serve it up with sippets[20] round the dish.

Of Artichoke Bottoms

Soak them in warm water for two or three hours, changing the water; then put them into the stew-pan with some good gravy, mushroom catsup, or powder Add a little Cayenne pepper, and salt when they boil thicken them with a little flour, put them into the dish with sauce over them, and serve them hot.

Of Calves' Sweet-breads

Scald[1] two or three sweet-breads, cut each into three or four pieces, and put them into a stew-pan with mushrooms, butter, and a faggot of sweet herbs; soak these together a moment, then add broth and gravy; simmer on a slow fire, skim the sauce well, and reduce it; season with pepper, salt, and lemon juice when ready

Of Roots

Cut carrots and parsnips to the length of a finger, and of much the same thickness; boil them till half done in water, put them into a stew-pan with small bits of ham, chopped parsley, and shalots, pepper and salt, a glass of wine and broth; let them stew slowly until the broth is reduced pretty thick, and add the squeeze of a lemon when ready to serve. For maigre[4] instead of ham, use mushrooms, and make a mixture beat up with yolks of egg and maigre broth. Celery is done much the same, only it is cut smaller. If these roots are to be served in a boat for sauce, boil them tender in the broth pot, or in water, cut them into the desired length, and serve with a good gravy or with white sauce.

MEATS &c.

TO BOIL MEATS, &C.

This most simple of culinary processes is not often performed in perfection, though it does not require so much nicety and attendance as roasting; to skim the pot well, and to keep it moderately boiling, and to know how long the joint requires, comprehends the most useful point of this branch of cookery. The cook must take especial care that the water really boils all the while she is cooking, or she will be deceived in the time. An adept cook will manage with much less fire for boiling than she uses for roasting, and to last all the time without much mending. When the water is coming to a boil there will always rise from the cleanest meat a scum to the top, this must be carefully taken off as soon as it appears, for on this depends the good appearance of a boiled dinner. When you have skimmed it well, put in a little cold water, which will throw up the rest of it. If let alone, it soons boils down and sticks to the meat, which, instead of looking white and healthful, will look coarse and uninviting.

Many cooks put in milk to make what they boil look white, but this does more harm than good; others wrap the meat in a cloth, but if it is well skimmed it will have a much more delicate appearance than when it is muffled up.

Put the meat into cold water in the proportion of about a quart to every pound of meat; it should remain covered during the whole process of boiling, but only just so. Water beyond what is absolutely necessary renders the meat less savoury and weakens the broth.

The water should be gradually heated according to the thickness, &c. of the article boiled; for instance, a leg of mutton of 10 lbs. weight should be placed over a moderate fire, which will gradually heat the water without causing it to boil, for about forty minutes. If the water boils much sooner, the meat will be hardened, and shrink up as if it were scorched. Reckon the time from its first coming to a boil; the slower it boils the tenderer, the plumper, and whiter it will be. For those who choose their food thoroughly cooked, twenty minutes to a pound will not be found too much for *gentle simmering* by the side of the fire. Fresh killed meat will take much longer time boiling than that which has been kept till what the butchers call ripe; if it be fresh killed it will be tough and hard if stewed ever so long, and ever so gently. The size of the boiling pots should be adapted to what they are to contain; in small families we recommend block tin[21] saucepans, &c. as lightest and safest, taking care that the covers fit close, otherwise the introduction of smoke may be the means of giving the meat a bad taste. Beef and mutton a little underdone is not a great fault, but lamb, pork, and veal are uneatable and truly unwholesome, if not thoroughly boiled. Take care of the liquor in which poultry or meat has been boiled, as an addition of peas, herbs, &c. will convert it into a nourishing soup.

TO BAKE MEATS, &C.

This is one of the cheapest and most convenient ways of dressing a dinner in small families, and although the general superiority of roasting must be allowed, still certain joints and dishes, such as legs and loins of pork, legs and shoulders of mutton and fillets of veal, will bake to great advantage, if the meat be good. Besides those joints above mentioned, we shall enumerate a few baked dishes which may be particularly recommended.

A pig when sent to the baker prepared for baking, should have its ears and tail covered with buttered paper, and a bit of butter tied up in a piece of linen to baste the back with, otherwise it will be apt to blister. If well baked it is considered equal to a roasted one.

A goose prepared the same as for roasting, or a *duck* placed upon a stand and turned, as soon as one side is done, upon the other, are equally good.

A buttock of beef, prepared as follows, is particularly fine: after it has been put in salt about a week, let it be well washed and put into a brown earthen pan with a pint of water; cover the pan tight over with 2 or 3 thicknesses of cap paper[22], and give it four or five hours in a moderately heated oven.

A ham, if not too old, put in soak for an hour, taken out and baked in a moderately heated oven, cuts fuller of gravy, and of a finer flavour, than a boiled one.

Cod fish, haddock, and *mackarel*, should have a dust of flour and some bits of butter spread over them. *Eels* when large and stuffed, *herrings* and *sprats,* are put in a brown pan, with vinegar and a little spice, and tied over with paper.

A hare, prepared the same as for roasting, with a few bits of butter and a little milk put into the dish and basted several times, will be found nearly equal to roasting: in the same manner *legs and shins of beef* will be equally good with proper vegetable seasoning.

TO ROAST MEATS, &C.

The first thing requisite for roasting is to have a strong steady fire, or a clear brisk one, according to the size and weight of the joint that is put down to the spit. A cook who does not attend to this, will prove herself totally incompetent to roast victuals properly. All roasting should be done open to the air, to ventilate the meat from its gross fumes, otherwise it becomes baked instead of roasted. The joint should be put down at such a distance from the fire as to imbibe the heat rather quickly, otherwise its plumpness and good quality will be gradually dried up, and it will turn shrively, and look meagre. When the meat is first put down, it is necessary to see that it balances well on the spit, otherwise the process of cooking will be very troublesome. When it is warm, begin to baste it well, which prevents the nutritive juices escaping;

and, if required, additional dripping must be used for that purpose.

As to sprinkling with salt while roasting, most able cooks dispense with it, as the penetrating particles of the salt have a tendency to draw out the animal juices; however, a little salt thrown on when first laid down, is sometimes necessary, with strong meats. When the smoke draws towards the fire, and the dropping of the clear gravy begins, it is a sure sign that the joint is nearly done. Then take off the paper, bast well, and dredge it with flour, which brings on that beautiful brownness which makes roasted meats look so inviting.

With regard to the time necessary for roasting various meats, it will vary according to the different sorts, the time it has been kept, and the temperature of the weather. In summer, 20 minutes may be reckoned equal to half an hour in winter. A good skreen to keep off the chilling currents of air, is essentially useful. The old housewife's rule is to allow rather more than a quarter of an hour to each pound, and in most instances it proves practically correct.

In roasting *mutton* or *lamb*, the loin, the chine, and the saddle, must have the skin raised, and skewered on; and when nearly done, take off this skin, and bast and flour to froth it up.

Veal requires roasting brown, and if a fillet or loin be sure to paper the fat, that as little of it may be lost as possible. When nearly done, baste it with butter and dredge with flour.

Pork should be well done. When roasting a loin cut the skin across with a sharp knife, otherwise the crackling is very awkward to manage. Stuff the knuckle part with sage and onion, and skewer it up. Put a little drawn gravy in the dish, and serve it up with apple sauce in a tureen. A spare-rib should be basted with a little butter, a little dust of flour, and some sage and onions shred small. Apple sauce is the only one which suits this dish.

Wild fowls require a clear brisk fire, and should be roasted till they are of a light brown, but not too much; yet it is a common fault to roast them till the gravy runs out, thereby losing their fine flavour.

Tame fowls require more roasting, as the heat is longer in penetrating: they should be often basted in order to keep up a strong froth, and to improve their plumpness.

Pigs and *geese* should be thoroughly roasted before

good fire, and turned quickly.

· *Hares and rabbits* require time and care, especially to have the ends sufficiently done, and to remedy that raw discolouring at the neck, &c., which proves often so objectionable at table.

TO REGULATE TIME IN COOKERY

Mutton

A leg of 8 lbs. will require two hours and a half.
A chine or saddle of 10 or 11 lbs. two hours and a half.
A shoulder of 7 lbs. one hour and a half.
A loin of 7 lbs. one hour and three-quarters.
A neck and breast, about the same time as a loin.

Beef

The sur-loin of 15 lbs. from three hours and three-quarters to four hours.
Ribs of beef, from 15 to 20 lbs. will take three hours to three hours and a half.

Veal

A fillet, from 12 to 16 lbs. will take from four to five hours, at a good fire.
A loin, upon the average, will take three hours.
A shoulder, from three hours to three hours and a half.
A neck, two hours.
A breast, from an hour and a half to two hours.

Lamb

Hind quarter of 8 lbs. will take from an hour and three-quarters, to two hours.
Fore-quarter of 10 lbs. about two hours.
Leg of 5 lbs. from an hour and a quarter, to an hour and a half.
Shoulder, or breast, with a quick fire, an hour.

Pork

A leg of 8 lbs. will require about three hours.
Griskin[23], an hour and a half.
A spare-rib of 8 or 9 lbs. will take from two hours and a half to three hours, to roast it thoroughly.
A bald spare-rib of 8 lbs. an hour and a quarter.
A loin of 5 lbs. if very fat, from two hours to two hours and a half.
A sucking pig, of three weeks old, about an hour and a half.

Poultry

A very large turkey will require about three hours; one of 10 lbs. two hours; a small one an hour and a half.
A full-grown fowl, an hour and a quarter; a moderate-sized one, an hour.
A pullet, from half an hour to 40 minutes.
A goose, full grown, from an hour and a half to two hours.
A green goose[24], 40 minutes.
A duck, full size, from 30 to 50 minutes.

Venison

A buck haunch which weighs from 20 to 25 lbs. will take about four hours and a half roasting: one from 12 to 18 lbs. will take three hours and a quarter.

TO BROIL

This culinary branch is very confined, but excellent as respects chops or steaks; to cook which in perfection, the fire should be clear and brisk, and the grid-iron[19] set on it slanting, to prevent the fat dropping in it. In addition, quick and frequent turning will ensure good flavour in the taste of the article cooked.

TO FRY MEATS, &C.

Be always careful to keep the frying-pan clean, and see that it is properly tinned. When frying any sort of fish, first dry them in a cloth, and then flour them. Put into the pan plenty of dripping, or hog's lard, and let it be boiling hot before putting in the fish. Butter is not so good for the purpose, as it is apt to burn and blacken, and make them soft. When they are fried, put them in a dish or hair sieve to drain, before they are sent to table. Olive oil is the best article for frying,

but it is very expensive, and bad oil spoils every thing that is dressed with it. Steaks and chops should be put in when the liquor is hot, and done quickly, of a light brown, and turned often. Sausages should be done gradually, which will prevent their bursting.

TO MAKE BEEF A LA MODE

Take 11 pounds of the mouse buttock, or clod of beef, cut it into pieces of 3 or 4 ounces each; put 2 or 3 large onions, and 2 ounces of beef dripping into a large deep stew-pan; as soon as it is quite hot, flour the meat, and put it into the stew-pan; fill it sufficiently to cover the contents with water, and stir it continually with a wooden spoon; when it has been on a quarter of an hour, dredge it with flour, and keep doing so till it has been stirred as much as will thicken it; then cover it with boiling water. Skim it when it boils, and put in 1 drachm[25] of black ground pepper, 2 of allspice, and 4 bay leaves; set the pan by the side of the fire to stew slowly about four hours. This is at once a savoury and economical dish.

TO MAKE A FRENCH STEW OF GREEN PEAS AND BACON

Cut about a quarter of a pound of fresh bacon into thin slices; soak it on the fire in a stew-pan until it is almost done; then put about a quart of peas to it,

a good bit of butter, a faggot of parsley, and 2 spoon ful of catsup; simmer on a slow fire and reduce t sauce: take out the faggot and serve the rest togethe

TO MAKE A SAVORY DISH OF VEAL

Cut some large scollops from a leg of veal, sprea them on a dresser, dip them in rich egg batter; seas them with cloves, mace, nutmeg, and pepper beate fine; make force-meat with some of the veal, some be suet, oysters chopped, sweet herbs shred fine; stre all these over the scollops, roll and tie them u put them on skewers and roast them. To the rest of t force-meat, add two raw eggs, roll them in balls, a fry them. Put them into the dish with the meat whe roasted; and make the sauce with strong broth, anchovy, or a shalot, a little white wine, and some spic Let it stew, and thicken it with a piece of butt rolled in flour. Pour the sauce into the dish, lay t meat in with the force-meat balls, and garnish wi lemon.

TO MAKE VEAL CAKE

Take the best end of a breast of veal, bone and cut in three pieces; take the yolks out of eight eg boiled hard, and slice the whites, the yolks to be c through the middle, two anchovies, a good de

18

of parsley chopped fine, and some lean ham cut in thin slices; all these to be well seasoned separately with Cayenne, black pepper, salt, and a little nutmeg; have ready a mug, the size of the intended cake, with a little butter rubbed on it, put a layer of veal on the bottom, then a layer of egg and parsley, and ham to fancy; repeat it till all is in, lay the bones on the top, and let it be baked three or four hours; then take off the bones and press down the cake till quite cold. The mug must be dipped into warm water, and the cake turned out with great care, that the jelly may not be broken which hangs round it.

TO MAKE DRY DEVILS

These are usually composed of the broiled legs and gizzards of poultry, fish bones, or biscuits, sauce piquante. Mix equal parts of fine salts, Cayenne pepper, and currie powder, with double the quantity of powder of truffles: dissect a brace of woodcocks rather under-roasted, split the heads, subdivide the wings, &c. &c. and powder the whole gently over with the mixture: crush the trail[26] and brains along with the yolk of a hard boiled egg, a small portion of pounded mace, the grated peel of half a lemon, and half a spoonful of soy, until the ingredients be brought to the consistence of a fine paste; then add a table-spoonful of catsup, a full wine glass of Madeira, and the juice of two Seville oranges; throw the sauce, along with the birds, into a stew-dish, to be heated with spirit of wine – cover close up – light the lamp – and keep gently simmering, and occasionally stirring, until the flesh has imbibed the greater part of the liquid. When it is completely saturated pour in a small quantity of salad oil, stir all once more well together, put out the light, and serve it round instantly.

TO MAKE AN OLIO

Boil in a broth-pot, a fowl, a partridge, a small leg of mutton, five or six pounds of large slices of beef, and a knuckle of veal; soak all these without broth for some time, turn the meat to give it a good colour, and add boiling water: when it has boiled about an hour, add all sorts of best broth herbs; this broth, when good, is of a fine brown colour.

TO POT LEG OF BEEF

Boil a leg of beef till the meat will come off the bone easily; then mix it with a cow heel, previously cut into thin pieces, and season the whole with salt and spice: add a little of the liquor in which the leg of beef was boiled, put it into a cheese-vat or cullender, or some other vessel that will let the liquor run off; place a very heavy weight over it, and it will be ready for use in a day or two. It may be kept in souse made of bran boiled in water, with the addition of a little vinegar.

TO POT BEEF

Cut it small, add to it some melted butter, 2 anchovies boned and washed, and a little of the best pepper, beat fine. Put them into a marble mortar, and beat them well together till the meat is yellow; put it into pots and cover with clarified butter.

TO POT EELS

Cut them in pieces about four inches long, season with a little beaten mace, nutmeg, pepper, salt and a little sal prunella[27], beaten fine. Lay them in a pan and pour as much clarified butter over as will cover it. Bake half an hour in a quick oven, till properly done. Then lay them on a coarse cloth to drain; when quite cold, season them again the same way. Then take off the butter they were baked in clear from the gravy of the fish, and set them in a dish before the fire. When melted, pour the butter over them and put by for use.

TO MAKE MOCK BRAWN

Take the head and belly piece of a young porker, well salt-petred[28]; split the head and boil it; take out the bones and cut it to pieces, then take four ox feet boiled tender, and cut them in thin pieces; lay them in the belly piece with the head cut small; roll it up tight with sheet tin, and boil it four or five hours. When it comes out set it up on one end, put a trencher[29] on it within the tin, press it down with a large weight, and let it stand all night. The next morning take it

out of the tin and bind it with a fillet, put it into cold salt and water, and it will be fit for use; it will keep a long time, if fresh salt and water are put into it every four days.

TO MAKE BOLOGNA SAUSAGES

Take a pound of beef suet, a pound of pork, a pound of bacon fat and lean, and a pound of beef and veal. Cut them very small. Take a handful of sage leaves chopped fine, with a few sweet herbs. Season pretty high with pepper and salt, take a large well-cleaned gut and fill it. Set on a saucepan of water, and when it boils, put it in, first pricking it to prevent its bursting. Boil it one hour.

TO MAKE EPPING SAUSAGES

Take 6 pounds of young pork, quite free from skin, gristle, or fat; cut it small, and beat it fine in a mortar. Chop 6 pounds of beef suet very fine, shred a handful of sage leaves fine, spread the meat on a clean dresser, and shake the sage over it. Shred the rind of a lemon very fine, and throw it with sweet herbs on the meat. Grate some nutmeg, to which put a spoonful of pepper, and a large spoonful of salt. Throw the suet over, and

mix all well together. Put it down close in the pot, and when it is to be used, roll it up with as much egg as will make it smooth.

TO MAKE SAVALOYS

Take 3 pounds of young pork free from bone and skin; salt it with an ounce of salt-petre[28], and a pound of common salt for two days; chop it fine; put in 3 tea-spoonsful of pepper; a dozen sage leaves chopped fine, and a pound of grated bread; mix it well, fill the guts, and bake them half an hour in a slack oven: they are good either hot or cold.

TO MAKE OXFORD SAUSAGES

Take one pound of young pork, fat and lean, without skin or gristle, 1 pound of beef suet, chopped fine together; put in ½ a pound of grated bread, half the peel of a lemon shred, a nutmeg grated, 6 sage leaves chopped fine, a tea-spoonful of pepper, and 2 of salt, some thyme, savory, and marjoram, shred fine. Mix well together and put it close down in a pan till used. Roll them out the size of common sausages, and fry them in fresh butter of a fine brown, or broil them over a clear fire, and send them to table hot.

PASTRIES &c.

TO MAKE A PUFF PASTE

Take a quarter of a peck[5] of flour, and rub it into a pound of butter very fine. Make it up into a light paste with cold water, just stiff enough to work it up. Then lay it out about as thick as a crown-piece; put a layer of butter all over, then sprinkle on a little flour, double it up, and roll it out again. Double and roll it with layers of butter, three times, and it will be fit for use.

TO MAKE A SHORT CRUST

Put six ounces of butter to eight ounces of flour, and work them well together; then mix it up with as little water as possible, so as to have it a stiffish paste; then roll it out thin for use.

TO MAKE A GOOD PASTE FOR LARGE PIES

Put to a peck[5] of flour three eggs, then put in half a pound of suet, a pound and a half of butter and suet, and as much of the liquor as will make it a good light crust. Work it up well and roll it out. Then cut it out in the desired form.

Another Method

Take a peck[5] of flour, and six pounds of butter, boiled in a gallon of water; then skim it off into the flour, with as little of the liquor as possible. Work it up well into a paste, pull it into pieces till cold, then make it into the desired form.

TO MAKE PASTE FOR TARTS

Put an ounce of loaf sugar, beat and sifted, to one pound of fine flour. Make it into a stiff paste, with a gill of boiling cream, and three ounces of butter. Work it well, and roll it very thin.

TO MAKE ORANGE CUSTARDS

Boil very tender the rind of half a Seville orange, and beat it in a mortar until it is very fine; put to it a spoonful of the best brandy, the juice of a Seville orange, four ounces of loaf sugar, and the yolk of four eggs. Beat them all together for ten minutes, and then pour in by degrees a pint of boiling cream; beat them until cold, then put them in custard cups, in a dish of hot water; let them stand till they are set, then take them out and stick preserved orange peel on the top; this forms a fine flavoured dish, and may be served up hot or cold.

BAKED CUSTARDS

Boil a pint of cream with some mace and cinnamon, and when it is cold, take four yolks of eggs, a little rose water, sack[30], nutmeg, and sugar, to taste; mix them well and bake them.

RICE CUSTARDS

Put a blade of mace, and a quartered nutmeg into a quart of cream; boil and strain it, and add to it some boiled rice and a little brandy. Sweeten it to taste,

stir it till it thickens, and serve it up in cups or in a dish; it may be used either hot or cold.

ALMOND CUSTARDS

Blanch a quarter of a pound of almonds, beat them very fine, and then put them into a pint of cream, with two spoonsful of rose water; sweeten it, and put in the yolks of four eggs; stir them well together till it becomes thick, and then pour it into cups.

LEMON CUSTARDS

Take half a pound of double refined sugar[31], the juice of two lemons, the rind of one pared very thin, the inner rind of one boiled tender and rubbed through a sieve, and a pint of white wine; boil them for some time, then take out the peel and a little of the liquor; strain them into the dish, stir them well together and set them to cool.

TO MAKE ALMOND TARTS

Blanch and beat fine some almonds, with a little white wine and some sugar (a pound of sugar to a pound of almonds), grated bread, nutmeg, cream, and the juice of spinach, to colour the almonds. Bake it in a gentle oven, and when done, thicken with candied orange peel or citron[32]

GREEN ALMOND TARTS

Pull the almonds from the tree before they shell, scrape off the down, and put them into a pan with cold spring water; then put them into a skillet[33] with more spring water; set it on a slow fire, and let it remain till it simmers. Change the water twice, and let them remain in the last till tender, then take them out and dry them well in a cloth. Make a syrup with double refined sugar[31], put them into it and let them simmer; do the same the next day, put them into a stone jar, and cover them very close, for if the least air comes to them they will turn black; the yellower they are before they are taken out of the water, the

greener they will be after they are done. Put them into the crust, cover them with syrup, lay on the lid, and bake them in a moderate oven.

TO MAKE ORANGE OR LEMON PIE

Rub six oranges or lemons with salt, and put them into water, with a handful of salt, for two days. Put every day fresh water without salt, for a fortnight. Boil them tender, cut them into half quarters, cornerways, quite thin: boil six pippins pared, cored, and quartered, in a pint of water till they break, then put the liquor to the oranges or lemons, with half the pulp of the pippins well broken, and a pound of sugar; boil them a quarter of an hour, then put them into a pot and squeeze in two spoonsful of the juice of either orange or lemon, according to the kind of tart; put puff paste, very thin, into shallow patty-pans. Take a brush, and rub them over with melted butter, sift double refined sugar[31] over them, which will form a pretty iceing, and bake them.

TO MAKE ORANGE TARTS

Grate a little of the outside of a Seville orange, squeeze the juice into a dish, put the peel into water, and change it often for four days, then put it into a saucepan of boiling water on the fire; change the water twice to take out the bitterness, and when tender, wipe and beat them fine in a mortar; boil their weight in double refined sugar[31] into a syrup, and skim it, then put in the pulp and boil all together till clear; when cold put it into the tarts, and squeeze in the juice, and bake them in a quick oven. Conserve of orange makes good tarts.

ORANGE PUFFS

Pare off the rinds from Seville oranges, then rub them with salt, let them lie twenty-four hours in water, boil them in four changes of water, make the first salt, drain and beat them to a pulp; bruise in the pieces of ali that are pared, make it very sweet with loaf-sugar, and boil it till thick; let it stand till cold, and then put it into the paste.

TO MAKE SNOW BALLS

Pare and take out the cores of five large baking apples, and fill the holes with orange or quince marmalade. Then take some good hot paste, roll the apples in it, and make the crust of an equal thickness; put them in a tin dripping pan, bake them in a moderate oven, and when taken out, make iceing for them; let the same be a quarter of an inch thick, and set them a good distance from the fire until they become hardened, but be cautious that they are not browned.

TO MAKE APPLE CAKES

Take half a quartern[34] of dough, roll it out thin; spread equally over it 5 ounces each of coffee and sugar, a little nutmeg or allspice, and 2 ounces of butter; then fold and roll it again two or three times, to mix well the ingredients. Afterwards roll it out thin, and spread over it 4 rather large apples, pared, cored, and chopped small; fold it up, and roll until mixed. Let it stand to rise after. Half a pound of butter may be added if desired.

TO MAKE FINE CHEESECAKES

Put a pint of warm cream into a saucepan over the fire, and when it is warm, add to it 5 quarts of new milk. Then put in some rennet, stir it, and when it is turned, put the curd into a linen cloth or bag. Let the whey drain from it, but do not squeeze it too much. Put it into a mortar, and pound it as fine as butter. Add ½ a pound of sweet almonds blanched, ½ a pound of macaroons, or Naples biscuit[35]. Then add nine well beaten yolks of eggs, a grated nutmeg, a little rose or orange water, and ½ a pound of fine sugar. Mix all well together.

ALMOND CHEESECAKES

Put 4 ounces of blanched sweet almonds into cold water, and beat them in a marble mortar or wooden bowl, with some rose water. Put to it 4 ounces of sugar, and the yolks of four eggs beat fine. Work it till it becomes white and frothy, and then make a rich puff paste as follows. Take ½ a pound of flour, and ¼ of a pound of butter; rub a little of the butter into the flour, mix it stiff with a little cold water, and then roll out the paste. Strew on a little flour and lay over it in thin bits one third of the butter, throw a little more flour over the bottom, and do the like three different times. Put the paste into the tins, grate sugar over them, and bake them gently.

BREAD CHEESECAKES

Slice a penny loaf as thin as possible, pour on it a pint of boiling cream, and let it stand two hours. Beat together 8 eggs, ½ a pound of butter, and grated nutmeg: mix them into the cream and bread with ½ a pound of currants well washed and dried, and a spoonful of white wine or brandy. Bake them in patty-pans, on a raised crust.

RICE CHEESECAKES

Boil 4 ounces of rice till it is tender, and then put it into a sieve to drain; mix with it 4 eggs well beaten up, ½ a pound of butter, ½ a pint of cream, 6 ounces of sugar, grated nutmeg, a glass of brandy, or ratafia water. Beat them all well together, then put them into raised crusts, and bake them in a moderate oven.

AN OMELETTE SOUFFLE

Put two ounces of the powder of chestnuts into a skillet[33], then add two yolks of new-laid eggs, and dilute the whole with a little cream, or even a little water; when this is done, and the ingredients well mixed, leaving no lumps, add a bit of the best fresh butter, about the size of an egg, and an equal quantity of powdered sugar; then put the skillet on the fire, and keep stirring the contents; when the cream is fixed and thick enough to adhere to the spoon, let it bubble up once or twice, and take it from the fire; then add a third white of an egg to those you have already set aside, and whip them to the consistency of snow: then amalgamate the whipped whites of eggs and the cream, stirring them with a light and equal hand, pour the contents into a deep dish, sift over with double

refined sugar[31], and place the dish on a stove with a fire over it as well as under, and in a quarter of an hour the cream will rise like an omelette souffle; as soon as it rises about four inches it is fit to serve up.

NOTTINGHAM PUDDING

Peel six good apples; take out the cores with the point of a small knife, but be sure to leave the apples whole; fill up where the core was taken from with sugar, place them in a pie dish, and pour over them a nice light batter; bake them an hour in a moderate oven.

DUTCH PUDDING

Cut a round piece out of the bottom of a Dutch loaf[36], and put that and the piece that was cut out into a quart of cold new milk, in the evening, and let it stand all night. If the milk is all soaked up by the morning, add some more. Put the piece into the bottom again, tie the loaf up in a cloth, and boil it an hour. Eat it with sugar, or with melted butter, white wine, and sugar sauce.

TO MAKE DR. KITCHENER'S PUDDING

Beat up the yolks and whites of three eggs, strain them through a sieve, and gradually add to them about a quarter of a pint of milk. Stir these well together; mix in a mortar, two ounces of moist sugar, and as much grated nutmeg as will lie on a sixpence; stir these into the eggs and milk. Then put in four ounces

of flour, and beat it into a smooth batter; stir 'in, gradually, eight ounces of very fine chopped suet, and three ounces of bread crumbs – mix all thoroughly together, at least half an hour before putting the pudding into the pot. Put it into an earthenware mould that is well buttered, and tie a pudding cloth over it.

TO MAKE BLANCMANGE

Put into 1 quart of water an ounce of isinglass[37], and let it boil till it is reduced to a pint, then put in the whites of 4 eggs with 2 spoonsful of rice water, and sweeten it to taste. Run it through a jelly bag, and then put to it 2 ounces of sweet, and 1 ounce of bitter almonds. Scald them in the jelly, and then run them through a hair sieve. Put it into a China bowl, and the next day turn it out. Garnish with flowers or green leaves, and stick all over the top blanched almonds cut lengthways.

CLEAR BLANCMANGE

Skim off the fat, and strain a quart of strong calf's foot jelly, add to the same the whites of 4 eggs well beaten, set it over the fire and stir it till it boils. Then pour it into a jelly bag, and run it through several times till it is clear. Beat an ounce each of sweet and bitter almonds to a paste with a spoonful of rose water strained through a cloth. Then mix it with the jelly, and add to it 3 spoonsful of very good cream. Set it again over the fire and stir it till it almost boils. Pour it into a bowl; then stir it often till almost cold; and then fill the moulds.

TO MAKE A DISH OF FRUMENTY

Boil an approved quantity of wheat; when soft, pour off the water, and keep it for use as it is wanted. The method using it is, to put milk to make it of an agreeable thickness; then warming it, adding some sugar and nutmeg.

TO MAKE A WINDSOR PUDDING

Shred half a pound of suet very fine, grate into it half a pound of French roll, a little nutmeg and the rind of a lemon. Add to these, half a pound of chopped apple, half a pound of currants, clean washed and dried, half a pound of jar raisins, stoned and chopped, a glass of rich sweet wine, and five eggs beaten with a little salt. Mill all thoroughly together, and boil it in a basin or mould, for three hours. Sift fine sugar over it when sent to table, and pour white wine sauce into the dish.

TO MAKE A PLAIN PUDDING

Weigh three-quarters of a pound of any odd scraps of bread, whether crust or crumb, cut them small, and pour on them a pint and a half of boiling water, to soak them well. Let it stand till the water is cool, then press it out, and mash the bread smooth with the back of a spoon. Add to it, a tea-spoonful of beaten ginger, some moist sugar, and three-quarters of a pound of currants. Mix all well together, and lay it in a pan well buttered. Flatten it down with a spoon, and lay some pieces of butter on the top. Bake it in a moderate oven, and serve it hot. When cold, it will turn out of the pan, and eat like good plain cheese cakes.

TANSY PUDDING

Blanch and pound a quarter of a pound of Jordan almonds; put them into a stew-pan, add a gill of the syrup of roses, the crumb of a French roll, some grated nutmeg, half a glass of brandy, two table-spoonsful of tansy juice, three ounces of fresh butter, and some slices of citron[32]. Pour over it a pint and a half of boiling cream, or milk, sweeten, and when cold, mix it; add the juice of a lemon, and eight eggs beaten. It may be either boiled or baked.

LEMON PUDDING

Cut off the rind of three lemons, boil them tender, pound them in a mortar, and mix them with a quarter of a pound of Naples biscuits[35], boiled up in a quart of milk or cream; beat up twelve yolks and six whites of eggs. Melt a quarter of a pound of fresh butter, and put in half a pound of sugar, and a little orange-flower water. Mix all well together, stir it over the fire, till thick, and squeeze in the juice of half a lemon. Put puff paste round the dish, then pour in the pudding; cut candied sweetmeats and strew over, and bake it for three-quarters of an hour.

TO MAKE RASPBERRY DUMPLINGS

Make a puff paste, and roll it out. Spread raspberry jam, and make it into dumplings. Boil them an hour; pour melted butter into a dish, and strew grated sugar over it.

QUINCE PUDDING

Scald[1] the quinces tender, pare them thin, scrape off the pulp, mix with sugar very sweet, and add a little ginger and cinnamon. To a pint of cream put three or four yolks of eggs, and stir it into the quinces till they are of a good thickness. Butter the dish, pour it in, and bake it.

TO MAKE A SOLID SYLLABUB

To a quart of rich cream put a quart of white wine, the juice of two lemons, with the rind of one grated and sweeten it to taste. Whip it up well and take off the froth as it rises. Put it upon a hair sieve and let it stand in a cool place till the next day. Then half fill the glasses with the scum, and heap up the froth as high as possible. The bottom will look clear and it will keep several days.

TO MAKE WHIPT SYLLABUB

Rub a lump of loaf sugar on the outside of a lemon, and put it into a pint of thick cream, and sweeten it to taste. Squeeze in the juice of a lemon, and add a glass of Madeira wine, or French brandy. Mill it to a froth with a chocolate mill[38], take off the froth as it rises, and lay it in a hair sieve. Fill one half of the glass with red wine, then lay the froth as high as possible, but take care that it is well drained in the sieve, or it will mix with the wine, and the syllabub be spoiled.

TO MAKE WHIPT CREAM

Mix the whites of eight eggs, a quart of thick cream, and half a pint of sack[30], sweeten them to taste with double refined sugar. It may be perfumed with a little musk[39] or ambergris[40] tied in a rag and steeped in a little cream. Whip it up with a whisk, and some lemon peel tied in the middle of the whisk. Then lay the froth with a spoon in the glasses, or basins.

TO MAKE ICE CREAM

To a pound of any preserved fruit add a quart of good cream, squeeze the juice of two lemons into it and some sugar to taste. Let the whole be rubbed through a fine hair sieve, and if raspberry, strawberry, or any red fruit, add a little cochineal to heighten the colour: have the freezing pot nice and clean; put the cream into it and cover it; then put it into the tub with ice beat small, and some salt; turn the freezing pot quick, and as the cream sticks to the sides, scrape it down with an ice-spoon, and so on till it is frozen. The more the cream is worked to the side with the spoon, the smoother and better flavoured it will be. After it is well frozen take it out and put it into ice shapes with salt and ice; then carefully wash the shapes for fear of any salt adhering to them; dip them in lukewarm water and send them to table.

RASPBERRY CREAM

Rub a quart of raspberries through a hair sieve, and take out the seeds, and mix it well with cream; sweeten it with sugar to your taste, then put it into a stone jug, and raise a froth with a chocolate mill[38]. As the froth rises, take it off with a spoon, and lay upon a hair sieve. When there is as much froth as wanted, put what cream remains in a deep China dish, and pour the frothed cream upon it, as high as it will lie on.

TO MAKE PISTACHIO CREAM

Beat half a pound of pistachio-nut kernels in a mortar with a spoonful of brandy. Put them into a pan with a pint of good cream and the yolks of two eggs beaten fine. Stir it gently over the fire till it grows thick, and then put it into a China soup plate. When it is cold stick it over with small pieces of the nuts, and send it to table.

CAKES

TO MAKE A RICH PLUM CAKE

Take one pound of fresh butter, one pound of sugar, one pound and a half of flour, two pounds of currants, a glass of brandy, one pound of sweetmeats, two ounces of sweet almonds, ten eggs, a quarter of an ounce of allspice, and a quarter of an ounce of cinnamon.

Melt the butter to a cream, and put in the sugar. Stir it till quite light, adding the allspice, and pounded cinnamon; in a quarter of an hour take the yolks of the eggs, and work them in, two or three at a time; and the whites of the same must by this time be beaten into a strong snow quite ready to work in, as the paste must not stand to chill the butter, or it will be heavy; work in the whites gradually; then add the orange peel, lemon, and citron[32], cut in fine stripes, and the currants, which must be mixed in well, with the sweet almonds. Then add the sifted flour and glass of brandy. Bake this cake in a tin hoop in a hot oven for three hours, and put twelve sheets of paper under it to keep it from burning.

A GOOD PLAIN CAKE

The following is a receipt for making a good plain cake, to be given to children, at breakfast, instead of buttered bread.

Take as much dough as will make a quartern[34] loaf (either made at home, or procured at the baker's), work into this a quarter of a pound of butter, a quarter of a pound of moist sugar, and a handful of caraway seeds. When well worked together, pull into pieces the size of a golden pippin, and work it together again. This must be done *three* times, or it will be in lumps, and heavy when baked.

TO MAKE ICEING FOR CAKES

Put one pound of fine-sifted, treble refined sugar[41] into a basin, and the whites of three new-laid eggs; beat the sugar and eggs up well with a silver spoon, until it becomes very white and thick; dust the cake over with flour, and then brush it off, by way of taking the grease from the outside, which prevents the iceing from running; put it on smooth with a palette knife, and garnish according to fancy: any ornaments should be put on immediately; for if the iceing gets dry, it will not stick on.

TO MAKE A RICH SEED CAKE

Take a pound and a quarter of flour well dried, a pound of butter, a pound of loaf sugar, beat and sifted, eight eggs and two ounces of caraway seeds, some grated nutmeg, and a spoonful of cinnamon. Beat the butter into a cream, put in the sugar, beat the whites of the eggs and the yolks separately, then mix them with the butter and sugar. Beat in the flour, spices, and seed, a little before sending it away. Bake it two hours in a quick oven.

RATAFIA CAKES

Beat half a pound each, of sweet and bitter almonds in fine orange, rose, or ratafia water, mix half a pound of fine pounded and sifted sugar with the same, add the whites of four eggs well beaten to it, set it over a moderate fire in a preserving-pan. Stir it one way until it is pretty hot, and when a little cool form it into small rolls, and cut it into thin cakes. Shake some

flour lightly on them, give each a light tap, and put them on sugar papers, sift a little sugar on them, and put them into a thorough slack oven.

TO MAKE WIGGS

Put half a pint of warm milk, to three-quarters of a pound of fine flour: mix in it two or three spoonsful of light yeast. Cover it up, and set it before the fire an hour, in order to make it rise. Work into it four ounces each, of sugar and butter, make it into cakes, or wiggs, with as little flour as possible, and a few caraway seeds, and bake them quick.

TO MAKE BATH CAKES

Mix well together, half a pound of butter, one pound of flour, five eggs, and a cupful of yeast. Set the whole before the fire to rise, which effected, add a quarter of a pound of fine powdered sugar, an ounce of caraways well mixed in, and roll the paste out into little cakes. Bake them on tins.

SHREWSBURY CAKES

Mix half a pound of butter well beat like cream, and the same weight of flour, one egg, six ounces of beaten and sifted loaf sugar, and half an ounce of caraway seeds. Form these into a paste, roll them thin, and lay them in sheets of tin; then bake them in a slow oven.

SAVOY CAKES

To one pound of fine sifted sugar, put the yolks of ten eggs, (have the whites in a separate pan) and set it, if in summer, in cold water: if there is any ice set the pan on it, as it will cause the eggs to be beat finer. Then beat the yolks and sugar well with a wooden spoon for 20 minutes, and put in the rind of a lemon grated; beat up the whites with a whisk, until they become quite stiff and white as snow. Stir them into the batter by degrees, then add three-quarters of a pound of well dried flour; and finally put it in a mould in a slack oven to bake.

A PLAIN POUND CAKE

Beat one pound of butter in an earthen pan until i is like a fine thick cream, then beat in nine whole egg till quite light. Put in a glass of brandy, a little lemo peel, shred fine, then work in a pound and a quarter o flour; put it into the hoop or pan and bake it for a hour. A pound plum cake is made the same wit putting one pound and a half of clean washed currant and half a pound of candied lemon peel.

TO MAKE PORTUGAL CAKES

Mix into a pound of fine flour, a pound of loaf sugar beat and sifted, and rub it into a pound of butter till it is thick, like grated white bread; then put to i two spoonsful of rose water, two of sack[30], and te eggs: work them well with a whisk, and put in eigh ounces of currants. Butter the tin pans, fill them hal full, and bake them. If made without currants the will keep a year.

SAFFRON CAKES

Take a quartern[34] of fine flour, a pound and a half o butter, three ounces of caraway seeds, six eggs, wel beaten, a quarter of an ounce of well-beaten clove and mace, a little pounded cinnamon, one pound o sugar, a little rose water and saffron, a pint and half of yeast, and a quart of milk. Mix them thus first boil the milk and butter, then skim off the butter and mix it with the flour and a little of the milk. Sti the yeast into the rest and strain it; mix it with th flour, put in the eggs and spice, rose water, tincture o saffron, sugar, and eggs. Beat it all well up, and bake i in a hoop or pan well buttered. Send it to a quic oven, and an hour and a half will do it.

QUEEN CAKES

Take a pound of sugar, beat and sift it, a pound o well dried flour, a pound of butter, eight eggs, and hal a pound of currants washed and picked; grate som nutmeg and an equal quantity of mace and cinnamon work the butter to a cream, put in the sugar, beat th

whites of the eggs 20 minutes, and mix them with the butter and sugar. Then beat the yolks for half an hour and put them to the butter. Beat the whole together, and when it is ready for the oven, put in the flour, spices, and currants; sift a little sugar over them, and bake them in tins.

RICE CAKES

Beat the yolks of 15 eggs for nearly half an hour, with a whisk, mix well with them 10 ounces of fine sifted loaf sugar, put in half a pound of ground rice, a little orange water or brandy, and the rinds of two lemons grated, then add the whites of seven eggs well beaten, and stir the whole together for a quarter of an hour. Put them into a hoop and set them in a quick oven for half an hour, when they will be properly done.

LEMON CAKES

Take one pound of sugar, three-quarters of a pound of flour, 14 eggs, two table-spoonsful of rose water, the raspings and juice of four lemons; when the yolks are well beat up and separated, add the powder sugar, the lemon raspings, the juice and the rose water; beat them well together in a pan with a round bottom, till it becomes quite light, for half an hour. Put the paste to the whites previously well whisked about, and mix it very light. When well mixed sift in the flour and knead it in with the paste, as light as possible; form the biscuits and bake them in small oval tins, with six sheets of paper under them, in a moderate heat. Butter the tins well or it will prove difficult to take out the biscuits, which will be exceedingly nice if well made. Ice them previous to baking, but very lightly and even.

TO MAKE BANBURY CAKES

Take a pound of dough made for white bread, roll it out, and put bits of butter upon the same as for puff paste, till a pound of the same has been worked in; roll it out very thin, then cut it into bits of an oval size, according as the cakes are wanted. Mix some good moist sugar with a little brandy, sufficient to wet it,

then mix some clean washed currants with the former, put a little upon each bit of paste, close them up, and put the side that is closed next the tin they are to be baked upon. Lay them separate, and bake them moderately, and afterwards, when taken out, sift sugar over them. Some candied peel may be added, or a few drops of the essence of lemon.

ALMOND CAKES

Take six ounces of sweet almonds, half a pound of powdered sugar, seven eggs, six ounces of flour, and the raspings of four lemons. Pound the almonds very fine, with whole eggs, add the sugar and lemon raspings, and mix them well together in the mortar. Take it out, put it in a basin and stir it with the yolks of eggs, till it is as white as a sponge paste; beat up the whites of the eggs to a strong snow, mix them very light with the paste, then take the flour and mix it as light as possible; on this the goodness of the paste principally depends, as it is impossible to make a good cake with a heavy paste; butter the mould and bake in a slack oven for an hour, with ten sheets of paper under it and one on the top.

TO MAKE PLAIN GINGERBREAD

Mix three pounds of flour with four ounces of moist sugar, half an ounce of powdered ginger, and one pound and a quarter of warm treacle; melt half a pound of fresh butter in it; put it to the flour and make it a paste; then form it into nuts or cakes, or bake it in one cake.

Another Method

Mix six pounds of flour with two ounces of caraway seeds, two ounces of ground ginger, two ounces of candied orange peel, the same of candied lemon peel cut in pieces, a little salt, and six ounces of moist sugar; melt one pound of fresh butter in about half a pint of milk, pour it by degrees into four pounds of treacle, stir it well together, and add it, a little at a time, to the flour; mix it thoroughly; make it into a

paste; roll it out rather thin, and cut into cakes with the top of a dredger or wine glass; put them on floured tins, and bake them in rather a brisk oven.

TO MAKE CREAM CAKES

Beat the whites of nine eggs to a stiff froth, stir it gently with a spoon lest the froth should fall, and to every white of an egg grate the rinds of two lemons; shake in gently a spoonful of double refined sugar[31] sifted fine, lay a wet sheet of paper on a tin, and with a spoon drop the froth in little lumps on it near each other. Sift a good quantity of sugar over them, set them in the oven after the bread is out, and close up the mouth of it, which will occasion the froth to rise. As soon as they are coloured they will be sufficiently baked; lay them by two bottoms together on a sieve, and dry them in a cool oven.

TO MAKE COMMON BUNS

Rub four ounces of butter into two pounds of flour, a little salt, four ounces of sugar, a dessert-spoonful of caraways, and a tea-spoonful of ginger: put some warm milk or cream to four table-spoonsful of yeast; mix all together into a paste, but not too stiff; cover it over and set it before the fire an hour to rise, then make it into buns, put them on a tin, set them before the fire for a quarter of an hour, cover over with flannel; then brush them with very warm milk, and bake them of a nice brown in a moderate oven.

TO MAKE CROSS BUNS

Put two pounds and a half of fine flour into a wooden bowl, and set it before the fire to warm; then add half a pound of sifted sugar, some coriander seed, cinnamon and mace powdered fine; melt half a pound of

butter in half a pint of milk, when it is as warm as can bear the finger, mix with it three table-spoonsf of very thick yeast, and a little salt; put it to the flou mix it to a paste, and make the buns as directed in th last receipt. Put a cross on the top, not very deep.

TO MAKE RUSKS

Beat up seven eggs, mix them with half a pint of warm new milk, in which a quarter of a pound of butter ha been melted, add a quarter of a pint of yeast, and thre ounces of sugar; put them gradually into as muc flour as will make a light paste nearly as thin as batter let it rise before the fire half an hour, add more flou to make it a little stiffer, work it well and divide into small loaves, or cakes, about five or six inche wide, and flatten them. When baked and cold p them in the oven to brown a little. These cakes whe first baked are very good buttered for tea; if they a made with caraway seeds they eat very nice cold.

TO MAKE CRUMPETS

Set two pounds of flour with a little salt before th fire till quite warm; then mix it with warm milk an water till it is as stiff as it can be stirred; let the mil be as warm as it can be borne with the finger, put cupful of this with three eggs well beaten, and mixe with three spoonsful of very thick yeast; then p this to the batter and beat them all well together in large pan or bowl, add as much milk and water as wi make it into a thick batter; cover it close and put before the fire to rise; put a bit of butter in a piece thin muslin, tie it up, and rub it lightly over the iro hearth or frying pan; then pour on a sufficient qua tity of batter at a time to make one crumpet; let do slowly, and it will be very light. Bake them all th same way. They should not be brown, but of a fi yellow colour.

CANDIES

TO PREPARE SUGAR FOR CANDYING

The first process is *clarifying*, which is done thus. Break the white of an egg into a preserving pan; put to it 4 quarts of water, and beat it with a whisk to a froth. Then put in 12 pounds of sugar, mix all together, and set it over the fire. When it boils put in a little cold water, and proceed as often as necessary, till the scum rises thick on the top. Then remove it from the fire, and when it is settled, take off the scum, and pass it through a straining bag. If the sugar should not appear very fine, boil it again before straining it.

TO CANDY SUGAR

After having completed the above first process, put what quantity is wanted over the fire, and boil it till it is smooth enough. This is known by dipping the skimmer into the sugar, and touching it between the forefinger and thumb; and immediately on opening them a small thread will be observed drawn between, which will crystallize and break, and remain in a drop on the thumb, which will be a sign of its gaining some degree of smoothness. Boil it again, and it will draw into a larger string; it is now called *bloom sugar*, and must be boiled longer than in the former process. To try its forwardness, dip again the skimmer shaking off the sugar into the pan; then blow with the mouth strongly through the holes, and if certain bladders go through, it has acquired the second degree; to prove if the liquid has arrived at the state called *feathered sugar*, re-dip the skimmer, and shake it over the pan, then give it a sudden flirt behind, and the sugar will fly off like feathers.

It now arrives to the state called *crackled sugar,*

to obtain which the mass must be boiled longer than in the preceding degree; then dip a stick in it, and put it directly into a pan of cold water, draw off the sugar which hangs to the stick in the water, and if it turns hard and snaps, it has acquired the proper degree of crystallization, if otherwise, boil it again until it acquires that brittleness.

The last stage of refining this article is called *caramel sugar*, to obtain which it must be boiled longer than in any of the preceding methods; prove it by dipping a stick first into the sugar, and then into cold water, and the moment it touches the latter it will, if matured, snap like glass. Be careful that the fire is not too fierce, as by flaming up the sides of the pan, it will burn, discolour, and spoil the sugar.

TO CANDY HOREHOUND[42]

Boil it in water until the juice is extracted: then boil a sufficient quantity of sugar to a great height, and add the juice to it. Stir it with a spoon against the sides of the sugar pan, till it begins to grow thick, then pour it out into a paper case that is dusted with fine sugar, and cut it into squares: dry the horehound, and put it into the sugar finely powdered and sifted.

TO MAKE BARLEY SUGAR

Take a quantity of clarified sugar in that state that on dipping the finger into the pan the sugar which adheres to it will break with a slight noise; this is called *crack*. When the sugar is near this, put in two or three drops of lemon juice, or a little vinegar to prevent its graining. When it has come to the *crack*,

take it off instantly, and dip the pan into cold water, to prevent its burning; let it stand a little, and then pour it on a marble which must be previously rubbed with oil. Cut the sugar into small pieces, when it will be ready for use. One drop of citron[32] will flavour a considerable quantity.

TO MAKE BON-BONS

Provide moulds, which must be of various shapes, and oiled with oil of sweet almonds. Take a quantity of brown sugar syrup in the proportion to their size, in that state called a *blow*, which may be known by dipping the skimmer into the sugar, shaking it, and blowing through the holes, when parts of light may be seen; add a drop of any esteemed essence. If the bon-bons are preferred white, when the sugar has cooled a little, stir it round the pan till it grains, and shines on the surface; then pour it into a funnel and fill the little moulds, when it will take a proper form and harden: as soon as it is cold, take it from the moulds; dry it two or three days, and put it upon paper. If the bon-bons are required to be coloured, add the colour just as the sugar is ready to be taken off the fire.

TO CANDY GINGER

Put 1 ounce of race[17] ginger grated fine, a pound of loaf sugar beat fine, into a preserving pan, with as much water as will dissolve the sugar. Stir them well together over a slow fire till the sugar begins to boil. Then stir in another pound of sugar, beat fine, and keep stirring it till it grows thick. Then take it off the fire, and drop it in cakes upon earthen dishes. Set them in a warm place to dry, when they will become hard and brittle, and look white.

TO CLARIFY LOAF SUGAR

Break the same into a copper pan, which will hold one third more, put half a pint of water to each pound of sugar, mix one white of egg to every 6 pounds; when it rises in boiling, throw in a little cold water, which must be kept ready in case it should boil over; skim it the fourth time of rising; continue to throw in a

little cold water each time till the scum ceases to rise, and strain it through a sieve, cloth or flannel bag. Save the scum, which when a certain quantity is taken off, may be clarified. The latter skimming will do to add to fermented wines.

TO CLARIFY COARSE BROWN SUGAR

Put 50 pounds of coarse brown sugar into a pan, which will contain one third more, pour in 20 pints of water, well mixed with 5 whites of eggs; pound 5 pounds of small charcoal, mix it in the pan while on the fire, and boil it till it looks as black as ink. If it rises too fast, add cold water, strain it through a bag, and though at first it will be black, continue to strain it until it becomes quite clear; which may be seen by putting the syrup in a glass. Put it back until it comes out as fine as clarified loaf sugar.

BIRCH SUGAR

Wound the trees in the spring of the year by boring a hole under a large arm of the tree quite through the wood as far as the bark of the opposite side; collect the sap which flows from the wound, and evaporate it to a proper consistence: these are the native sugars of cold countries, and might be made in England for all the purposes of home consumption.

TO MAKE PEAR SUGAR

It is obtained by expressing the juice, adding chalk to remove the superabundant acid, and evaporating it to a due consistence; it does not crystallize, and is a kind of white treacle. One hundred weight of apples yields about 84 pounds of this juice, which will produce nearly 12 pounds of this substance.

TO CANDY ORANGE PEEL

Soak the peels in cold water, which change frequently till they lose their bitterness; then put them into syrup till they become soft and transparent. Then they are to be taken out and drained.

TO PRESERVE CANDIED ORANGE FLOWERS

Free them from their cups, stamina, and pistils, put four ounces into one pound of sugar boiled to a candy height, and poured on a slab, so as to be formed into cakes.

TO MAKE CANDIED ANGELICA

The stalks are to be boiled for a quarter of an hour in water, to take away their bitterness, and some of the strong scent; they are then to be put into syrup, boiled to a full candied height, and kept on the fire until they appear quite dry, and then they are to be taken out and drained.

TO MAKE CANDIED ERYNGO[43]

Is prepared nearly in the same manner as candied angelica, but the roots are only slit, and washed three or four times in cold water, before they are put into the syrup.

TO COLOUR CANDIED SUGAR

Red

Boil an ounce of cochineal in half a pint of water for 5 minutes, add an ounce of cream of tartar, half an ounce of pounded alum[44], and boil them on a slow fire 10 minutes; if it shews the colour clear on white paper, it is sufficient. Add two ounces of sugar, and bottle for use.

Blue

Put a little warm water in a plate, and rub an indigo-stone[45] in it till the colour has arrived at the tint which is required.

Yellow

Rub with some water a little gamboge[46] on a plate, or infuse the heart of a yellow lily flower, with milk-warm water.

Green

Boil the leaves of spinach about a minute in a little water, and, when strained, bottle the liquor for use. In colouring refined sugars, taste and fancy must guide.

TO MAKE DEVICES IN SUGAR

Steep gum-tragacanth[47] in rose water, and with double refined sugar[31] make it into a paste, and colour and mould it to fancy.

TO MAKE CONFECTIONARY DROPS

Take double refined sugar[31], pound and sift it through a hair sieve, not too fine; then sift it through a silk sieve, to take out all the fine dust, which would destroy the beauty of the drop. Put the sugar into a clean pan, and moisten it with any favourite aromatic; if rose water, pour it in slowly, stirring it with a paddle, which the sugar will fall from, as soon as it is moist enough, without sticking. Colour it with a small quantity of liquid carmine[48], or any other colour, ground fine. Take a small pan with a lip, fill it three parts with paste, place it on a small stove, the half hole being of the size of the pan[49], and stir the sugar with a little ivory or bone handle, until it becomes liquid. When it almost boils, take it from the fire and continue to stir it: if it be too moist, take a little of the powdered sugar, and add a spoonful to the paste, and stir it till it is of such a consistence as to run without too much extension. Have a tin plate, very clean and smooth; take the little pan in the left hand, and hold in the right a bit of iron, copper, or silver wire, four inches long, to take off the drop from the lip of the pan, and let it fall regularly on the tin plate; two hours afterwards, take off the drops with the blade of a knife.

TO MAKE CHOCOLATE DROPS

Scrape the chocolate to powder, and put an ounce to each pound of sugar; moisten the paste with clear water, work it as above, only take care to use all the paste prepared, as if it be put on the fire a second time, it greases, and the drop is not of the proper thickness.

TO MAKE ORANGE-FLOWER DROPS

These are made as the sugar drops, only using orange-flower water, or, instead of it, use the essence of naroli[50], which is the essential oil of that flower.

COFFEE DROPS

An ounce of coffee to a pound of sugar will form a strong decoction[51]: when cleared, use it to moisten the sugar, and then make the drops as above.

GINGER DROPS

Pound and sift through a silk sieve the required quantity of ginger, according to the strength wanted, and add it to the sugar with clear water. China ginger is best, being aromatic as well as hot and sharp tasted.

CLOVE DROPS

These are made as cinnamon drops, the cloves being pounded, or the essence used. Good cloves should be black, heavy, of a pungent smell, hot to the taste, and full of oil.

TO MAKE EXTRACT OF LIQUORICE

The liquorice root is to be boiled in eight times its weight of water, to one half; the liquor is then to be expressed, and, after the fæces have subsided, to be filtered; it is then to be evaporated, with a heat between 200° and 212° Fahrenheit, until it becomes thickish; and, lastly, it is to be evaporated with a heat less than 200°, and frequently stirred, until it acquires a consistence proper for forming pills. This is made into little pastilles, or flat cakes, often bearing the impression of the places where they are made; and a bit now and then put into the mouth, takes off the tickling of a cough. It should be sucked to make it pleasant, as much of the juice taken at a time is unpleasant.

TO MAKE LIQUORICE LOZENGES

Take of extract of liquorice, double refined sugar[31], each 10 oz; tragacanth[47], powdered, 3 oz. Powder thoroughly, and make into lozenges with rose water.

These are agreeable pectorals[52], and may be used at pleasure in tickling coughs. The above receipt is the easiest and best mode of making these lozenges. Refined extract of liquorice should be used: and it is easily powdered in the cold, after it has been laid for some days in a dry and rather warm place.

CONSERVES

TO CANDY ORANGE MARMALADE

Cut the clearest Seville oranges into two, take out all the juice and pulp into a basin, and pick all the skins and seeds out of it. Boil the rinds in hard water till they become tender, and change the water two or three times while they are boiling. Then pound them in a marble mortar, and add to it the juice and pulp; put them next into a preserving pan with double their weight in loaf sugar, and set it over a slow fire. Boil it rather more than half an hour, put it into pots: cover it with brandy paper [53], and tie it close down.

TO MAKE TRANSPARENT MARMALADE

Cut very pale Seville oranges into quarters, take out the pulp, put it into a basin, and pick out the skins and seeds. Put the peels into a little salt and water, and let them stand all night, then boil them in a good quantity of spring water until they are tender; cut them in very thin slices, and put them into the pulp. To every pound of marmalade put one pound and a half of double refined [31] beaten sugar; boil them together gently for 20 minutes; if they are not transparent, boil them a few minutes longer. Stir it gently all the time, and take care not to break the slices. When it is cold, put the marmalade into jelly and sweetmeat glasses tied down tight.

BARBERRY [54] MARMALADE

Mash the barberries in a little water, on a warm stove; pass them through a hair sieve with a paddle: weigh the pulp and put it back on the fire; reduce it to one half, clarify a pound of sugar and boil it well; put in the pulp, and boil it together for a few minutes.

QUINCE MARMALADE

Take quinces that are quite ripe, pare and cut them in quarters, take out the cores, put them in a stew-pan with spring water, nearly enough to cover them, keep them closely covered and let them stew gently till they are quite soft and red, then mash and rub them through a hair sieve. Put them in a pan over a gentle fire, with as much thick clarified sugar as the weight of the quinces; boil them an hour and stir the whole time with a wooden spoon to prevent its sticking; put it into pots and when cold tie them down.

TO MAKE SCOTCH MARMALADE

Take of the juice of Seville oranges, 2 pints, and yellow honey, 2 lbs. Boil to a proper consistence.

TO MAKE HARTSHORN [55] JELLY

Boil half a pound of hartshorn in three quarts of water over a gentle fire till it becomes a jelly; when a little hangs on a spoon it is done enough. Strain it hot, put it into a well-tinned saucepan, and add to it half a pint of Rhenish wine [56], and a quarter of a pound of loaf sugar. Beat the whites of four eggs or more to a froth, stir it sufficiently for the whites to mix well with the jelly, and pour it in as if cooling it. Boil it two or three minutes, then put in the juice of four lemons, and let it boil two minutes longer. When

it is finely curdled and of a pure white, pour it into a swan-skin jelly bag over a China basin, and pour it back again until it becomes as clear as rock water; set a very clean China basin under, fill the glasses, put some thin lemon rind into the basin, and when the jelly is all run out of the bag, with a clean spoon fill the rest of the glasses, and they will look of a fine amber colour. Put in lemon and sugar agreeable to the palate.

TO MAKE CURRANT JELLY

Take the juice of red currants, 1 lb., and sugar, 6 oz. Boil down.

Another Method

Take the juice of red currants, and white sugar, equal quantities. Stir it gently and smoothly for three hours, put it into glasses, and in three days it will concrete into a firm jelly.

BLACK CURRANT JELLY

Put to ten quarts of ripe dry black currants, one quart of water; put them in a large stew-pot, tie paper close over them, and set them for two hours in a cool oven. Squeeze them through a fine cloth, and add to every quart of juice a pound and a half of loaf sugar broken into small pieces. Stir it till the sugar is melted; when it boils skim it quite clean. Boil it pretty quick over a clear fire, till it jellies, which is known by dipping a skimmer into the jelly and holding it in the air; when it hangs to the spoon in a drop, it is done. If the jelly is boiled too long it will lose its flavour and shrink very much. Pour it into pots, cover them with brandy papers[53], and keep them in a dry place. Red and white jellies are made in the same way.

APPLE JELLY

Take of apple juice strained, 4 lbs., sugar, one pound. Boil to a jelly.

STRAWBERRY JELLY

Take of the juice of strawberries, 4 lbs., sugar, 2 lbs.

GOOSEBERRY JELLY

Dissolve sugar in about half its weight of water, and boil: it will be nearly solid when cold; to this syrup add an equal weight of gooseberry juice, and give it a boil but not long, for otherwise it will not fix.

RASPBERRY JAM

Mash a quantity of fine ripe dry raspberries, strew on them their own weight of loaf sugar, and half their weight of white currant juice. Boil them half an hour over a clear slow fire, skim them well, and put them into pots or glasses; tie them down with brandy papers[53], and keep them dry. Strew on the sugar as quick as possible after the berries are gathered, and in order to preserve their flavour they must not stand long before boiling them.

STRAWBERRY JAM

Bruise very fine some scarlet strawberries, gathered when quite ripe, and put to them a little juice of red currants. Beat and sift their weight in sugar, strew it over them, and put them into a preserving pan. Set them over a clear slow fire, skim them, and then boil them for twenty minutes, and finally put them into glasses.

PRESERVING

Some rules are necessary to be observed in this branch of confectionery. In the first place, observe in making syrups that the sugar is well pounded and dissolved, before it is placed on the fire, otherwise their scum will not rise well, nor the fruit obtain its fine colour. When stone fruit is preserved, cover them with mutton suet rendered[57], to exclude the air, which is sure ruin to them. All wet sweetmeats must be kept dry and cool to preserve them from mouldiness and damp. Dip a piece of writing paper in brandy, lay it close to the sweetmeats, cover them tight with paper, and they will keep well for any length of time; but will inevitably spoil without these precautions.

Another Method

The fruit, if succulent, either prepared or not, is first soaked for some hours in very hard water, or in a weak alum[44] water; pour syrup, boiled to a candy height, and half cold, over the fruit; after some hours, the syrup, weakened by the sauce of the fruit, is to be poured off, re-boiled, and poured on again; and this repeat several times. When the syrup is judged to be no longer weakened, the fruit is to be taken out of it, and well drained.

TO BOTTLE DAMSONS

Put damsons, before they are too ripe, into wide-mouthed bottles, and cork them down tight; then put them into a moderately heated oven, and about three hours more will do them; observe that the oven is not too hot, otherwise it will make the fruit fly. All kinds of fruits that are bottled may be done in the same way,

and they will keep two years; after they are done, they must be put away with the mouth downward, in a cool place, to keep them from fermenting.

TO PRESERVE BARBERRIES[53]

Set an equal quantity of barberries and sugar in a kettle of boiling water, till the sugar is melted and the barberries quite soft; let them remain all night. Put them next day into a preserving pan, and boil them fifteen minutes, then put them into jars, tie them close, and set them by for use.

TO PRESERVE GRAPES

Take close bunches, whether white or red, not too ripe, and lay them in a jar. Put to them a quarter of a pound of sugar candy, and fill the jar with common brandy. Tie them up close with a bladder, and set them in a dry place.

TO PRESERVE SEVILLE ORANGES WHOLE

Cut a hole at the stem end of the oranges, the size of sixpence, take out all the pulp, put the oranges into cold water, for two days, changing it twice a day; boil them rather more than an hour, but do not cover them, as it will spoil the colour; have ready a good syrup, into which put the oranges, and boil them till they look clear; then take out the seeds, skins, &c. from the pulp first taken out of the oranges, and add to it one of the whole oranges, previously boiled, with an equal weight of sugar to it and the pulp; boil this

together till it looks clear over a slow fire, and when cold fill the oranges with this marmalade, and put on the tops; cover them with syrup, and put brandy paper[53] on the top of the jar. It is better to take out the inside at first, to preserve the fine flavour of the juice and pulp, which would be injured by boiling in the water.

TO DRY CHERRIES

Having stoned the desired quantity of morello cherries, put a pound and a quarter of fine sugar to every pound; beat and sift it over the cherries, and let them stand all night. Take them out of their sugar, and to every pound of sugar, put two spoonsful of water. Boil and skim it well, and then put in the cherries; boil the sugar over them, and next morning strain them, and to every pound of syrup put half a pound more sugar; boil it till it is a little thicker, then put in the cherries and let them boil gently. The next day strain them, put them in a stove, and turn them every day till they are dry.

TO PRESERVE FRUITS IN BRANDY OR OTHER SPIRITS

Gather plums, apricots, cherries, peaches, and other juicy fruits, before they are perfectly ripe, and soak them for some hours in hard, or alum[44] water, to make them firm; as the moisture of the fruit weakens the spirit, it ought to be strong, therefore add five ounces of sugar to each quart of spirit.

TO PRESERVE STRAWBERRIES WHOLE

Take an equal weight of fruit and double refined sugar[31], lay the former in a large dish, and sprinkle half the sugar in fine powder; give a gentle shake to the dish, that the sugar may touch the under side of the fruit. Next day make a thin syrup with the remainder of the sugar; and allow one pint of red currant juice, to every three pounds of strawberries; in this simmer them until sufficiently jellied. Choose the larges scarlets, not dead ripe.

TO PRESERVE APRICOTS

Infuse young apricots before their stones become hard, into a pan of cold spring water, with plenty of vine leaves; set them over a slow fire until they are quite yellow, then take them out and rub them with a flannel and salt to take off the lint; put them into the pan to the same water and leaves, cover them close at a distance from the fire, until they are a fine light green, then pick out all the bad ones. Boil the best gently two or three times in a thin syrup, and let them be quite cold each time before you boil them. When they look plump and clear, make a syrup of double refined sugar[31], but not too thick; give your apricots a gentle boil in it, and then put them into the pots or glasses, dip a paper in brandy, lay it over them, tie them close, and keep them in a dry place.

TO KEEP GOOSEBERRIES

Put an ounce of roche alum[58] beat very fine, into a large pan of boiling hard water; place a few gooseberries at the bottom of a hair sieve, and hold them in the water till they turn white. Then take out the sieve, and spread the gooseberries between two cloths put more into the sieve, then repeat it, till they are all done. Put the water into a glazed pot until the next day, then put the gooseberries into wide-mouthed bottles; pick out all the cracked and broken ones, pour the water clear out of the pot, and fill the bottles with it, cork them loosely and let them stand a fortnight. If they rise to the corks, draw them out and let them stand two or three days uncorked; and then cork them up close again.

PICKLING

This branch of domestic economy comprises a great variety of articles, which are essentially necessary to the convenience of families. It is at the same time too prevalent a practice to make use of brass utensils to give pickle a fine colour. This pernicious custom is easily avoided by heating the liquor and keeping it in a proper degree of warmth before it is poured upon the pickle. Stone jars are the best adapted for sound keeping. Pickles should never be handled with the fingers, but by a spoon kept for the purpose.

TO PICKLE ONIONS

Put a sufficient quantity into salt and water for nine days, observing to change the water every day; next put them into jars and pour fresh boiling salt and water over them, cover them close up till they are cold, then make a second decoction[51] of salt and water, and pour it on boiling. When it is cold drain the onions on a hair sieve, and put them into wide-mouthed bottles; fill them up with distilled vinegar; put into every bottle a slice or two of ginger, a blade of mace, and a tea-spoonful of sweet oil, which will keep the onions white. Cork them well up in a dry place.

TO MAKE SAUR KRAUT

Take a large strong wooden vessel, or cask, resembling a salt-beef cask, and capable of containing as much as is sufficient for the winter's consumption of a family. Gradually break down or chop the cabbages (deprived of outside green leaves) into very small pieces; begin with one or two cabbages at the bottom of the cask, and add others at intervals, pressing them by means of a wooden spade, against the side of the cask, until it is full. Then place a heavy weight upon the top of it, and allow it to stand near to a warm place, for four or five days. By this time it will have undergone fermentation, and be ready for use. Whilst the cabbages are passing through the process of fermentation, a very disagreeable fetid, acid smell is exhaled from them; now remove the cask to a cool situation, and keep it always covered up. Strew aniseeds among the layers of the cabbages during its preparation, which communicates a peculiar flavour to the Saur Kraut at an after period.

In boiling it for the table, two hours are the period for it to be on the fire. It forms an excellent nutritious and antiscorbutic[59] food for winter use.

TO MAKE PECCALILLI, INDIAN METHOD

This consists of all kinds of pickles mixed and put into one large jar – girkins, sliced cucumbers, button onions, cauliflowers broken in pieces. Salt them, or put them in a large hair sieve in the sun to dry for three days, then scald[1] them in vinegar a few minutes; when cold put them together. Cut a large white cabbage in quarters, with the outside leaves taken off and cut fine, salt it, and put it in the sun to dry for three or four days; then scald it, the same as cauliflower and carrots – three parts boiled in vinegar, and a little bay salt; French beans, samphire[60], reddish pods[61], and masturchions[62], all go through the same process as girkins, capsicums, &c. To one gallon of vinegar put four ounces of ginger bruised, two ounces of whole white pepper, two ounces of allspice, half an ounce of chillies bruised, four ounces of turmeric, one pound of the best mustard, half a pound of shalots,

one ounce of garlic and half a pound of bay salt. The vinegar, spice and other ingredients, except the mustard, must boil half an hour; then strain it into a pan, put the mustard into a large basin, with a little vinegar; mix it quite fine and free from lumps, then add more; when well mixed put it to the vinegar just strained off, and when quite cold put the pickles into a large pan, and the liquor over them; stir them repeatedly so as to mix them all; finally, put them into a jar, and tie them over first with a bladder, and then with leather. The capsicums want no preparation.

TO PICKLE CUCUMBERS

Let them be as free from spots as possible; take the smallest that can be got, put them into strong salt and water for nine days, till they become yellow; stir them at least twice a day; should they become perfectly yellow, pour the water off and cover them with plenty of vine leaves. Set the water over the fire, and when it boils, pour it over them, and set them upon the earth[63] to keep warm. When the water is almost cold make it boil again, and pour it upon them; proceed thus till they are of a fine green, which they will be in four or five times; keep them well covered with vine leaves, with a cloth and dish over the top to keep in the steam, which will help to green them.

When they are greened put them in a hair sieve to drain, and then to every two quarts of white wine vinegar put half an ounce of mace, ten or twelve cloves, an ounce of ginger cut into slices, an ounce of

black pepper, and a handful of salt. Boil them all together for five minutes; pour it hot on the pickles, and tie them down for use. They may also be pickled with ale, ale vinegar, or distilled vinegar, and adding three or four cloves of garlic and shalots.

TO PICKLE ARTIFICIAL ANCHOVIES

To a peck[5] of sprats put two pounds of salt, three ounces of bay salt, one pound of salt-petre[28], two ounces of prunella[27], and a few grains of cochineal; pound all in a mortar, put into a stone pan first a layer of sprats, and then one of the compound, and so on alternately to the top. Press them down hard; cover them close for six months, and they will be fit for use, and will really produce a most excellent flavoured sauce.

TO PICKLE MUSHROOMS

Put the smallest that can be got into spring water, and rub them with a piece of new flannel dipped in salt. Throw them into cold water as they are cleaned, which will make them keep their colour; next put them into a saucepan with a handful of salt upon them. Cover them close and set them over the fire four or five minutes, or till the heat draws the liquor from them; next lay them betwixt two dry cloths till they are cold; put them into glass bottles and fill them up with distilled vinegar, with a blade of mace, and a tea-

spoonful of sweet oil into every bottle; cork them up close and set them in a dry cool place; as a substitute for distilled vinegar, use white wine vinegar, or ale. Allegan[64] will do, but it must be boiled with a little mace, salt, and a few slices of ginger, and it must be quite cold before it is poured upon the mushrooms.

Another Method

Bruise a quantity of well-grown flaps of mushrooms with the hands, and then strew a fair proportion of salt over them; let them stand all night, and the next day put them into stew-pans; set them in a quick oven for twelve hours, and strain them through a hair sieve. To every gallon of liquor put of cloves, Jamaica black pepper, and ginger, one ounce each, and half a pound of common salt; set it on a slow fire, and let it boil till half the liquor is wasted: then put it into a clean pot, and when cold bottle it for use.

TO PICKLE WALNUTS WHITE

Pare green walnuts very thin till the white appears, then throw them into spring water with a handful of salt, keep them under water six hours, then put them into a stew-pan to simmer five minutes, but do not let them boil; take them out and put them in cold water and salt; they must be kept quite under the water with a board, otherwise they will not pickle white, then lay them on a cloth and cover them with another to dry; carefully rub them with a soft cloth and put them into the jar, with some blades of mace and nutmeg sliced thin. Mix the spice between the nuts and pour distilled vinegar over them; when the jar is full of nuts pour mutton fat over them, and tie them close down with a bladder and leather.

TO PICKLE SAMPHIRE[60]

Put what quantity wanted into a clean pan, throw over it two or three handsful of salt, and cover it with spring water for twenty-four hours; next put it into a clean saucepan, throw in a handful of salt, and cover it with good vinegar. Close the pan tight, set it over a slow fire, and let it stand till the samphire is green and crisp; then take it off instantly, for should it remain till it is soft, it will be totally spoiled. Put it into the pickling pot and cover it close, when it is quite cold tie it down with a bladder and leather, and set it by for use. Samphire may be preserved all the year by keeping it in a very strong brine of salt and water, and just before using it, put it for a few minutes into some of the best vinegar.

TO PICKLE SALMON

Boil the fish gently till done, and then take it up, strain the liquor, add bay leaves, peppercorns, and salt; give these a boil, and when cold add the best vinegar to them; then put the whole sufficiently over the fish to cover it, and let it remain a month at least..

TO PRESERVE FISH BY SUGAR

Fish may be preserved in a dry state, and perfectly fresh, by means of sugar alone, and even with a very small quantity of it.

Fresh fish may be kept in that state for some days, so as to be as good when boiled as if just caught. If dried, and kept free from mouldiness, there seems no limit to their preservation; and they are much better in this way than when salted. The sugar gives no disagreeable taste.

This process is particularly valuable in making what is called kippered salmon; and the fish preserved in this manner are far superior in quality and flavour to those which are salted or smoked. If desired, as much salt may be used as to give the taste that may be required; but this substance does not conduce to their preservation.

In the preparation, it is barely necessary to open the fish, and to apply the sugar to the muscular parts, placing it in a horizontal position for two or three days, that this substance may penetrate. After this it may be dried; and it is only further necessary to wipe and ventilate it occasionally, to prevent mouldiness.

A table-spoonful of brown sugar is sufficient in this manner for a salmon of five or six pounds weight; and if salt is desired, a tea-spoonful or more may be added. Salt-petre[28] may be used instead, in the same proportion, if it is desired to make the kipper hard.

TO SALT HAMS

For three hams pound and mix together, half a peck[5] of salt, half an ounce of salt prunella[27], three ounces of salt-petre[28], and four pounds of coarse salt; rub the hams well with this, and lay what is to spare over them, let them lie three days, then hang them up. Take the pickle in which the hams were, put water enough to cover the hams with more common salt, till it will bear an egg, then boil and skim it well, put it in the salting tub, and the next morning put it in the hams; keep them down the same as pickled pork; in a fortnight take them out of the liquor, rub them well with brine, and hang them up to dry.

TO DRY SALT BEEF AND PORK

Lay the meat on a table or in a tub with a double bottom, that the brine may drain off as fast as it forms, rub the salt well in, and be careful to apply it to every niche; afterwards put it into either of the above utensils, when it must be frequently turned; after the brine has ceased running, it must be quite buried in salt, and kept closely packed. Meat which has had the bones taken out is the best for salting. In some places the salted meat is pressed by heavy weights or a screw, to extract the moisture sooner.

TO PICKLE IN BRINE

A good brine is made of bay salt and water, thoroughly saturated, so that some of the salt remains undissolved; into this brine the substances to be preserved are plunged, and kept covered with it. Among vegetables, French beans, artichokes, olives, and the different sorts of samphire[60], may be thus preserved, and among animals, herrings.

To Salt by Another Method

Mix brown sugar, bay salt, common salt, each two pounds, salt-petre[28] eight ounces, water two gallons; this pickle gives meats a fine red colour, the sugar renders them mild and of excellent flavour. Large quantities may be managed by these proportions.

A MISCELLANY

TO IMPROVE AND INCREASE SUGAR

To 5 pounds of coarse brown sugar, add 1 pound of flour, and there will be obtained 6 pounds of sugar worth 10 per cent more in colour and quality.

TO CLARIFY HONEY

The best kind is clarified by merely melting it in a water bath, and taking off the scum; the middling kind by dissolving it in water, adding the white of an egg to each pint of the solution, and boiling it down to its original consistence, skimming it from time to time. The inferior kind requires solution in water, boiling the solution with one pound of charcoal, to 25 pounds of honey, adding, when an excess of acid is apprehended, a small quantity of chalk or oyster shell powder; next by straining it several times through flannel, and reducing the solution to its original consistence by evaporation.

TO PRESERVE SEEDS IN HONEY FOR VEGETATION

Seeds of fruits, or thin stalk strips, may be preserved by being put into honey; and on being taken out, washed, and planted, they will vegetate kindly.

TEA

By some, the use of this exotic is condemned in terms the most vehement and unqualified, while others have either asserted its innocence, or gone so far as to ascribe to it salubrious, and even extraordinary virtues. The truth seems to lie between these extremes: there is however an essential difference in the effects of *green tea* and of *black*, or *bohea*; the former of which is much more apt to affect the nerves of the stomach than the latter, more especially when drank without cream, and likewise without bread and butter. That, taken in a large quantity, or at a later hour than usual, tea often produces watchfulness, is a point that cannot be denied; but if used in moderation, and accompanied with the additions just now mentioned, it does not sensibly discover any hurtful effects, but greatly relieves an oppression of the stomach and abates a pain of the head. It ought always to be made of a moderate degree of strength: for if too weak it certainly relaxes the stomach. As it has an astringent taste, which seems not very consistent with a relaxing power, there is ground for ascribing this effect not so much to the herb itself as to the hot water, which not being impregnated with a sufficient quantity of tea, to correct its own emollient tendency, produces a relaxation, unjustly imputed to some noxious quality of the plant. But tea, like every other commodity, is liable to damage, and when this happens, it may produce effects not necessarily connected with its original qualities.

COFFEE

It is allowed that coffee promotes digestion, and exhilarates the animal spirits; besides which, various other qualities are ascribed to it, such as dispelling flatulency, removing dizziness of the head, attenuating viscid humours, increasing the circulation of the blood, and consequently perspiration; but if drank too strong, it affects the nerves, occasions watchfulness,

and tremor of the hands; though in some phlegmatic constitutions it is apt to produce sleep. Indeed, it is to persons of that habit that coffee is well accommodated: for to people of a thin and dry habit of body it seems to be injurious. Turkey coffee is greatly preferable in flavour to that of the West Indies. Drank, only in the quantity of one dish, after dinner to promote digestion, it answers best without either sugar or milk; but if taken at other times, it should have both; or in place of the latter rather cream, which not only improves the beverage, but tends to mitigate the effect of coffee upon the nerves.

A SUBSTITUTE FOR MILK AND CREAM

Beat up the whole of a fresh egg, in a basin, and then pour boiling tea over it gradually, to prevent its curdling. It is difficult from the taste to distinguish the composition from rich cream.

TO MAKE ICE

The following is a simple and speedy method of congealing water. Into a metal vase half filled with water, pour very gently an equal quantity of ether, so that no mixture may take place of the two liquids. The vase is placed under the receiver of an air-pump, which is so fixed upon its support as to remain quite steady when the air is pumped out. At the first strokes of the piston, the ether becomes in a state of ebullition; it is evaporated totally in less than a minute, and the water remains converted into ice.

TO STORE FRUIT

Those to be used first, lay by singly on shelves, or on the floor, in a dry southern room, on clean dry moss, or sweet dry straw, so as not to touch one another. Some, or all the rest, having first laid a fortnight singly, and then nicely culled, are to be spread on shelves, or on a dry floor. But the most superior way is, to pack in large earthen, or China or stone jars with very dry long moss at the bottom, sides, and also between them, if it might be. Press a good coat of moss on the top, and then stop the mouth close with cork, or otherwise, which should be rosined round about with a 20th part of bees' wax in it. As the object is effectually to keep out air, (the cause of putrefaction), the jars, if earthen, may be set on dry sand, which put also between, round, and over them, to a foot thick on the top. In all close storing, observe there should be no doubt of the soundness of the fruit. Guard, in time, from frost those that lie open. Jars of fruit must be soon used after unsealing.

SLEEP AFTER MEALS

It is a disputed point, whether a short sleep after dinner be not useful for promoting digestion; and in several countries the practice certainly is indulged with impunity, if not with evident advantage; besides that it seems to be consistent with the instinct of nature. It is however, only among a certain class that the practice can be used with propriety; and whoever adopts it, ought to confine the indulgence to a short sleep of a few minutes. For, if it be continued longer, there arises more loss, from the increase of insensible perspiration, than can be compensated by all the advantages supposed to accrue to digestion.

Those who use such a custom, which may be allowable to the aged and delicate, ought to place themselves in a reclining, not a horizontal posture; because in the latter situation the stomach presses upon a part of the intestines, and the blood is consequently impelled to the head.

Glossary

1. **To scald:** to pour boiling water over food in order to facilitate cleaning, removal of hairs etc., or to heat almost to boiling point

2. **Pinion:** part of a bird's wing corresponding to the forearm

3. **Savoy:** a pale green crinkly variety of cabbage

4. **Maigre:** usually meaning not containing flesh or the juices of flesh. May also mean "meagre"

5. **Peck:** measure of capacity for dry ingredients equal in cubic content to 2 gallons

6. **Tulips:** probably turnips

7. **Laurel leaf:** leaf from the bay tree, the true laurel *Laurus nobilis* (not *Prunus laurocerasus,* the leaves of which are poisonous)

8. **Purslain:** common or garden purslane, *Portulaca oleracea*

9. **Burnet:** Great Burnet, *Sanguisorba officinalis*

10. **Bugloss:** Viper's Bugloss, *Echium vulgare*

11. **Liver-wort:** American liverwort, *Anemone hepatica,* or English liverwort, *Peltigera camina*

12. **Fumitory:** herb, *Fumaria officinalis*

13. **Rocambole:** a species of onion with the flavour of garlic

14. **Cullis:** strong broth made from meat or poultry boiled and strained

15. **Verjuice:** the acid liquor obtained from sour grapes, crab apples or other sour fruit

16. **Long pepper:** condiment prepared from dried unripe fruit-spikes of the pepper plants – *Piper officinarum* and *P. longum*

17. **Races:** roots

18. **Grass:** asparagus

19. **Gridiron:** metal frame on which meat or fish is broiled (or grilled) usually over a charcoal fire

20. **Sippets:** small pieces of bread, fried or roasted, used for garnishing, like croutons

21. **Block tin:** tin which is refined and cast in ingots

22. **Cap paper:** a kind of wrapping or filter paper

23. **Griskin:** lean part of the loin of a bacon pig

24. **Green goose:** a goose killed when young (less than four months old) and eaten without stuffing

25. **Drachm:** one sixteenth of an ounce

26. **Trail:** the entrails and intestines of certain birds and fish. (Usually cooked and eaten with the flesh.)

27. **Sal prunella:** preparation of fused potassium nitrate in balls

28. **Salt-petre:** potassium nitrate

29. **Trencher:** wooden, metal or earthenware platter for serving meat, etc.

30. **Sack:** types of dry, amber-coloured wine from Spain and the Canaries. Sherry would be the equivalent

31. **Double refined sugar:** caster sugar

32. **Citron:** a fruit similar to lemon, but larger, less acid and with a thicker skin

33. **Skillet:** small metal saucepan with a long handle, often with legs for placing over fire

34. **Quartern:** standard weight of a loaf of bread, in those days about 4 lbs.

35. **Naples biscuit:** a plain biscuit used as a substitute for breadcrumbs

36. **Dutch loaf:** a loaf of characteristic shape, originating from Holland.

37. **Isinglass:** comparatively pure type of gelatine obtained from the air-bladders of freshwater fish, especially sturgeon

38. **Chocolate mill:** utensil for mixing the chocolate and milk when preparing a chocolate drink

39 Musk: aromatic substance obtained from a bag-like gland of the male musk deer

40 Ambergris: odoriferous wax-like substance secreted in intestines of sperm-whale

41 Treble refined sugar: icing sugar

42 Horehound: white horehound, *Marrubium vulgare*

43 Eryngo: sea holly, *Eryngium maritimum*

44 Alum: a compound salt formerly employed as an improving agent in bread and for fixing dyes. In 1848 it was pronounced "dangerous", and its use in food was banned in the first Food and Drugs Act, 1860

45 Indigo-stone: a substance obtained from plants of the genus Indigofera, now processed and sold in the form of powder or granules

46 Gamboge: a gum resin taken from the tree, *Garcinia hanburyii*, which may be found in Siam, Cambodia and Ceylon

47 Gum-tragacanth: gum taken from the shrub *Astragalus gummifer* which grows in western Asia

48 Carmine: crimson colouring derived from cochineal

49 i.e. use the plate on the stove which fits the size of the pan; this prevents undue loss of heat and the sugar is less likely to burn

50 Naroli: neroli, oil of orange blossom, *Citrus aurantium*

51 Decoction: the liquor resulting from the extraction of the soluble parts from a substance by boiling

52 Pectorals: medicines, etc., good for diseases of the chest

53 Brandy paper: piece of writing or cap paper, dipped in brandy

54 Barberry: red, oblong acid fruit of the shrub, *Berberis vulgaris*

55 Hartshorn: matter obtained from inside the horns of the hart, formerly the chief source of ammonia, and used as smelling salts in its liquid form

56 Rhenish wine: wine from the Rhine area, hock

57 Mutton suet rendered: the dripping extracted by melting down fat from meat

58 Roche alum: rock alum (see also Alum[44])

59 Antiscorbutic: preventing scurvy

60 Samphire: *Crithmum maritimum*, plant with fleshy aromatic leaves, found on rocky coasts in Europe

61 Reddish pods: the dried pods of Capsicum or Red Pepper (when powdered these form the basis of Cayenne Pepper)

62 Masturchions: nasturtiums, of which the seeds are often pickled

63 Earth: hearth

64 Allegan: probably "alegar" – sour ale or malt vinegar

Index